CAUGHT
IN THE
MIDDLE

CAUGHT
IN THE
MIDDLE

Monkeygate, Politics and
Other Hairy Issues;

the Autobiography of Mike Procter

By Mike Procter
and Lungani Zama

First published by Pitch Publishing, 2017

Pitch Publishing
A2 Yeoman Gate
Yeoman Way
Worthing
Sussex
BN13 3QZ
www.pitchpublishing.co.uk
info@pitchpublishing.co.uk

A CIP catalogue record is available for this book
from the British Library.

ISBN 978-1-78531-216-8

Typesetting and origination by Pitch Publishing

Printed in Great Britain by TJ International.

Contents

Acknowledgements

DECIDING TO write a book is no easy thing, and it certainly requires a team effort. I am hugely indebted to Paul and Jane Camillin, of Pitch Publishing, for agreeing to go ahead with the book, and for being patient with all the late changes and updates. I owe Lungani Zama, my co-writer, a huge thanks, for his hours and hours of dedication and transcribing, and countless drives from Maritzburg to Durban North, as we put everything together. To Mark Nicholas, a friend who agreed on writing a foreword without a moment's hesitation, my sincere thanks.

And finally, to all those who helped put this entire project together, sourcing pictures and stats from the old days, and making sense of it all. Without all of your help, none of this would have been possible.

Foreword by Mark Nicholas

THERE IS a great sadness in South African cricket and it filters through its past. Fine cricketers, interspersed with truly great ones, are not recognised by the body that runs the modern game. With a vengeful eye, Cricket South Africa refuse to acknowledge men such as Aubrey Faulkner, Dudley Nourse, Johnny Waite, Hugh Tayfield, Graeme Pollock, Barry Richards and Mike Procter, all of whom have been denied a cap number, and refused any visible legacy. This is like saying to a young German that the two wars did not happen, or arguing that there was no America before the abolition of slavery; no Australia before Indigenous Australians had a vote.

History is fact. What is done is done. Apartheid was no fault of the cricketers: indeed, some of those cricketers paid a high price for the policies of the government of the time. But they were not of the government of the time themselves.

Cricket South Africa's position is not just unfair, it's daft. History offers the chance for both reflection and inspiration. Present players need to know about past players so that their place in the order of things is understood and valued. At the moment, the official line on South African cricket is that it started in 1991, when re-admitted to the ICC after 21 years of global isolation. But it didn't, it started in 1889 with a Test against England and, more than 400 Tests later, it is still going strong.

Procter is one who has suffered from this humiliation. He never grumbles, saying simply 'What can you do?' Of course, deep down it hurts for there is no more of a cricketing man, and a South African one at that. But he cracks on – forever 'Proccie', whose sanity remains by virtue of friends made the world over, a glass of something cold and shared memories of a game so loved.

Think of the Procter CV: South Africa, Natal, Western Province, Rhodesia and Gloucestershire; Rest of the World, World Series Cricket and captain of the South African XI in the first years of the rebel tours; coach or director of cricket at international, provincial and county levels; international match referee; commentator for four networks worldwide; chairman of the national selection panel – 'And I never lost a match at Lord's!' he proudly says.

He scored six consecutive hundreds in the Currie Cup, bowled the speed of light when the mood took him, swung the ball a mile, ripped his off-breaks and held most catches that came his way. He played the game in a buccaneering style, entertaining crowds and terrifying opponents. When the day was done, foe became friend and the night was young. Only a few have carried this off. Legend has it that Keith Miller played with the gods in sunlight and after dark, Sir Garry Sobers too. Another cricketing knight, Sir Ian Botham was of similar stock. Well, put Proc on the list too and if you think that an exaggeration, ask anyone around at the time.

There is no choosing the greatest all-rounder, frankly it's a mug's game. Those who saw him say it's Sobers, end of story. Figures tell us Jacques Kallis is top dog. Tony Greig's record has him surprisingly near the top of the charts. Perhaps only Imran Khan truly warranted a place with both bat and ball for the most part of his career but it's impossible to know what any of these formidable cricketers might have achieved in one discipline without the other. Is it more, or less? Could Kapil Dev or Botham have batted with such abandon had they not bowled with such success? Do the wickets taken by Richard Hadlee and Shaun Pollock do enough to carry their erratic batting? Shall we include the stumpers – Alan Knott and Adam Gilchrist – in the debate? And so on.

Perhaps Botham single-handedly won more matches than any other. Maybe Proc would have matched him because his game adapted to so many different surfaces and conditions. The point about Proccie is that he excelled at every turn. He was a hero, of mine and millions of others. He was inspiration and is often reflection. His legacy is too important to be ignored.

Now he brings us up to date with a book, and what a story there is to tell. A man at the centre of so much and in the middle of so much more. During his time with various administrations, he has been both well supported and hung out to dry. The role of match referee stretched him fully and, at times, went beyond his simple truths – such is the occasionally underhand nature of the modern game. The whole point about Proc is the simple truths, alongside the glorious talents. I'd have paid to watch him play, indeed I did. I impersonated his quirky action, made to cream fully-pitched balls over mid-off and extra cover and even copied his style of speech. And now I'll read the book. Onwards Michael John, and bravo!

Mark Nicholas
London, March 2017

Mike Procter and Me

**An introduction by John Saunders,
the man Mike Procter calls 'the best
coach I ever had'.**

I WAS 15 and small for my age. For several years I had had but one ambition: to play cricket for South Africa. I saw myself following in the tradition of the legendary Balaskas, the leg-spin googly bowler who – a year before I had been born – had bowled South Africa to their first ever victory on English soil. Xenophon Balaskas. A name redolent with magic and mystery. A name to conjure with. At Hilton College I spent every available free moment bowling in the nets. In lessons I was seldom without a cricket ball, holding it, feeling it, spinning it in my fingers. At night I would dream of leg spin bowling. My ambition to play for South Africa was shared by my closest friend, Howard – an off-spin bowler. I had changed from off-spin to leg-spin bowling three years before, and could bowl a sharply turning leg break, two googlies (one disguised) and a top spinner. All I lacked was regular match practice and a modicum of control.

Then came the big moment – the day which was to change my life – a Sunday in the South African summer of 1951. I had been invited by my housemaster, Robin Routledge (in his day a leg-spin bowler) to play in the school staff cricket team against a club called Hillcrest. Routledge was nicknamed 'Spook' (Afrikaans for 'ghost') because his expression never changed. Rumour had it that when a boy at Hilton he had been wildly anarchic but that he had suffered shell-shock while serving in the Second World War. I was pleased to be taken under his unsmiling wing.

It was an away match. Hillcrest played on the Highbury Preparatory School cricket field and in the pavilion were photographs and memorabilia of some of the school's great Test cricketers. Next to the ground lived the legendary Wally Hammond. But – at least initially – there was no hint of cricketing greatness in the home team.

They won the toss and chose to bat. Their batting did not look strong and I anticipated an early return back to Hilton. They had an opening batsman who looked and played rather like a crab and who survived the onslaught of our team's fast bowlers through a combination of dogged defence and good luck. At the other end, wickets fell regularly.

Judging from the shots of the top order batsmen, I decided that Hillcrest must be a farming community. At 56 for 4, the Spook signalled to me to prepare to take the next over. My friend Howard was in the process of bowling a maiden to 'the Crab'. Batsman number six, to whom I was about to bowl, had just come in and was still to face a ball. He was a thick-set man with a slight limp. I decided that he was probably the start of the tail and that in a rural community none of numbers 6 to 11 would have had much experience of playing against leg-spin, let alone googly bowling. What happened next remains in my memory as a vivid blur.

My first ball was a perfectly flighted leg break which pitched on middle stump. My burly opponent hit across the line, skying the ball to 'cow corner', where my English teacher (nicknamed 'Bog-brush') stumbled, failed to take the catch, and allowed the ball to trickle over the boundary. A very near miss. My next ball was slightly over-pitched and the batsman hit it cleanly out of the ground over the midwicket pavilion. 'Good shot, Woodrow', said the Crab. It took a scowling Bog-brush several minutes to retrieve and return the ball. Spook, standing at mid-off, looked on impassively. In South Africa, in 1951, an over consisted of eight balls. I had six more to bowl. They included two over-pitched leg breaks, an under-pitched googly and a somewhat wild attempt at top spin – each of which found Bog-brush and a small army of spectators foraging for the ball in the small valley which lay beyond the pavilion. I had had enough. My last two balls were bowled as fast as I could bowl and were aimed well outside the off stump. The batsman, revealing that he was more than just a farmer with a good eye, produced two brutal lofted cover drives which added 12 more to his score. Forty-six runs had been scored off me in a single over.

'Take a breather,' said the Spook. At the other end a smirking Howard bowled yet another maiden over to the Crab. I gave way to a medium-pace trundler, whose first over went for 32. In three overs, one a maiden, Hillcrest had moved from 56 to 132. Woodrow Procter went on to make a big hundred and, following the declaration, revealed that he too was a leg-spin bowler, skittling out the Hilton College Staff XI – who had little experience of facing leg-spin bowling – for about 50. That was to be my last ever attempt at leg-spin bowling. On the following Monday I awoke as a born-again off-spinner – second in line of succession to my friend Howard.

I met Woodrow Procter again just three years later. After a year at university studying medicine and fearing failure and the wrath of my parents, I had accepted a post as a very young assistant master at the same Highbury School – where I was soon in charge of coaching rugby and cricket. In the summer, I turned out for the Hillcrest cricket side and found that I was Woodrow's spin twin. We often bowled in tandem – my flat accurate off-spin a foil to his more deadly leg-spin and googly bowling. Woodrow was no agriculturalist. At the age of 16, he had been a schoolboy prodigy – selected to play for Eastern Province and thought to be a certainty as one of the South African team, which, but for the outbreak of war, would have visited Australia in 1939.

He had returned from the war with a knee injury which kept him out of serious cricket. In 1955, his ambitions were centred on the cricketing futures of his two sons, Anton and Michael. Soon, I too had a new ambition – to assist in producing South African cricketers of the future. And initially I had an unexpected assistant – Wally Hammond, who had agreed to help me with the coaching of the school first XI. Hammond was an unrelenting and rather grumpy perfectionist. For one afternoon a week he attempted to teach every boy under his scrutiny to bat the way he did. For the other four afternoons a week, I tried to teach the team to bat with gay abandon – the way I did. Hammond did not suffer fools – or unorthodox batsmen – gladly and he abandoned his coaching after a single term.

Once established as the school's only first XI coach, I easily persuaded Woodrow to send Mike, his youngest son, to Highbury. Even at the age of ten, Mike was prodigiously talented, modelling himself on his father. He bowled leg-spin with good rhythm and control and showed a wonderful eye for a moving ball, having little need to rely much on technique. When Mike became a member of the school first XI, I was faced with a dilemma. It seemed clear to me that he should abandon the dreadfully precarious, all-consuming, trade of leg-spin bowling and concentrate on his batting. Eventually I was able to convince his father of the wisdom of this judgement and, for nearly two years, Mike played in the first XI as a wicketkeeper/batsman.

In his last term at Highbury, Mike began to bowl fast in the nets. He bowled so fast that I was easily persuaded to allow him to abandon wicketkeeping. Inter-school rivalries were intense and with Mike batting sublimely and bowling at great speed the team was invincible. He seemed to bowl off the wrong foot – perhaps a legacy of his leg-spinning days. In 1959, his last year at Highbury, Mike broke every school batting record – most memorably scoring a double hundred against an XI representing the cream of Johannesburg's preparatory schools. He went on from Highbury to Hilton and not long after he was opening the bowling for South Africa and playing an important part in SA's whitewashing of the then world champions, Australia. He had emerged on the world stage as a bowling all-rounder.

Looking back through an old Highbury School magazine, I find that I wrote this on Mike's contribution to the 1959 season:

> He would appear to be the best player Highbury have ever had, and this year he developed a willingness to learn which he had previously lacked. Against Transvaal Primary Schools, he scored a brilliant 210* without playing one careless shot. He could be a very good wicketkeeper, but at the moment prepares to bowl and concentrate on his batting. This is Procter the cricketer, but Procter the boy is more remarkable. He was the most modest player in the side, and the first to praise goodness in others. If he snicks a ball, he walks out whether the umpire has seen it or not. A century or a duck, he takes the game with the same cheery smile.

Looking back on those early days, I realise that though Mike's cricketing talent and his combativeness undoubtedly owed much to Woodrow, his father, his serene, generous and cheery temperament probably owed much to his mother.

After retiring from first-class cricket Mike continued to make a contribution as a coach and international umpire. In his writings and in interviews he has been surprisingly lacking in bitterness.

When asked what he felt about the politics which had removed South Africa from the world stage and forced him to become something of a 'cricketing buccaneer', he replied:

> What is a Test career compared to the suffering of 40 million people? Lots of people lost a great deal more in those years, and if by missing out on a Test career we played a part in changing an unjust system, then that is fine by me.

For the last five years, Mike, inspired by two quotations from his hero, Nelson Mandela, has devoted time, money and expertise to assist in providing a better life for the children of Ottawa Primary School – an establishment close to Durban. The two Mandela quotations are: 'Sport has the power to change the world' and 'We owe our children, the most vulnerable citizens in any society, a life free from violence and fear'.

Chapter 1

An untimely blast

THE DAY of 8 May 2002 will always sit in my memory as one of the most surreal of my entire life. On the face of it, that Wednesday morning should have been just like any other, save for the fact that the second Test between Pakistan and New Zealand was starting that day in Karachi.

Pakistan had won the first Test quite easily, with Shoaib Akhtar producing some of the fasted bowling I had ever seen. The Black Caps, managed by Jeff Crowe, were expected to make a stiffer fist of it in the second Test. As it turned out, they never got the chance, and were on the plane back to New Zealand before the end of one of the most dramatic days of my life – and I have had a few!

It was just after 8am that morning when things took a wicked turn for the worse. Pakistan has always been one of my favourite cricket nations; all the people are fanatical about the game, the weather is hot – a bit like Durban, where I played most of my cricket – and their national team always seems to find a way to be entertaining.

This was my first tour as an international match referee, and completed a career in the game that had started as a player, then coach, international team manager, commentator and now, match referee. Cricket had been my life for just about all of my life, and I wouldn't have wanted it any other way.

The one-day series had preceded the Test matches, and aside from a bit of crowd disturbance which had been sorted out with the help of the home skipper, Moin Khan, things had gone along pretty smoothly. After a long and mostly fruitful association with the sport, I had figured that being a match referee was going to be the least frenetic of tasks, aside from the comfort of the commentary box, of course!

How wrong I was. At around 8:15am, having just finished breakfast with the match umpires, I was in my room on the sixth floor of our hotel, when an incredible noise froze me in fear. The force of the blast shattered the glass from my window back into the room, and the whole building felt like it was shaking for a few seconds.

As we were to later find out, a suicide bomb had gone off in a car outside the hotel next to us, tearing apart a bus and, such was the force of it all, it really felt like it had come from somewhere below us, in the same building. Luckily, none of the players or the officials were too badly hurt, as everyone was just preparing to go downstairs to the buses that were waiting to take us to the ground.

I distinctly remember walking down the stairs, as we couldn't take the lift, and passing someone who had apparently suffered a mini heart attack. Thankfully, they had been attended to by then, but things were significantly worse outside. On the street, the scene was like something out of a war movie. There were body parts strewn all over, as well as parts of cars and the hotel building itself. It was horrific, but as the match referee, I had to try and take some sort of control of the situation, and ensure the players' safety. The Kiwis were pretty shaken up. Their physio, Dayle Shackel, had been struck by bits of glass because he was standing too close to his window at the time of the blast. Having consulted the International Cricket Council (ICC), I then called a hasty meeting with the team managers and captains, and informed them that the tour had been abandoned.

New Zealand, understandably, were in no state to continue, and that left Pakistan with very few alternatives. I can still remember how distraught the Pakistan Cricket Board (PCB) director at the time, Brig Munawar Rana, was. He kept on apologising, saying that he had let everyone down. Of course, it wasn't his fault at all. You can plan for most things in the world, but you can never predict the evil thoughts of a few rotten apples.

That entire morning was such a blur, and I still couldn't tell you how long the time lapse was from the moment the bomb went off, to the time we were on our way to the airport, instead of the ground for the first morning. Everything whizzed by, but there was simply no way that we could have stayed a minute longer. By the time we got on the plane, we had been informed that 11 French nationals, working on submarine projects, had been killed.

The entire incident had nothing to do with cricket, but it immediately changed the face of the game. To their great credit, and the relief of the Pakistan people and its cricket board, New Zealand returned in the 2003/04 season to fulfil their tour obligations. Sadly, that 2002 incident wasn't an isolated incident, and the 2009 attack on the Sri Lankan team bus in Lahore meant the end of tours to Pakistan.

Sitting on the plane going back to South Africa, it was all still sinking in. Whatever ideas I had about match refereeing being a nice way to end my long love affair with the game had been violently shaken out of me and, in hindsight, I guess my very first tour as an international match referee should have been a warning for what was to come over the next five years on the job.

Having enjoyed a playing career of nearly 20 years, where I often had little time to consider consequences and played purely on instinct, I was soon to learn that it wasn't just impulsive batsmen who could be caught on the fence. As a referee, you were always in the middle, and the decisions you made sometimes had huge implications.

As I have gone on to find out, some implications actually stick with you for life.

Chapter 2

India, a place for new beginnings

1991 WAS a historic year for South African cricket. After decades of being dormant, we got the recall from the International Cricket Council, thanks to the sustained efforts of Dr Ali Bacher and his team. It was incredibly exciting, and the next big thing for us was to go off on the first tour abroad, to India. There were to be no Test matches, but it didn't matter one jot to us. We were travelling somewhere as representatives of South Africa, and that alone was huge. We were replacing Pakistan as opponents at the last minute, of course, and it was funny to see some tickets that still stated India–Pakistan on them. Their cancellation was a godsend to us, of course, and we took it with both hands.

For some reason, I remember being a little concerned about what kit we would be wearing for the trip to India. It was the first time a South African touring team had come together in two decades, and it would have been the last thing on anyone's mind to design one. In the midst of getting passports and visas, never mind actually picking a team, worrying about kit was probably a bit random, but it certainly sticks in my mind.

Of course, the real headache for me as a coach was what team was going over to India. Immediately, I wanted Clive Rice to be my captain, and Ali agreed completely. Ricey was perfect for the situation; he was experienced, and he had the respect of all of the players. As an all-rounder, Ricey could also contribute to the cause with bat and ball and, though he had lost a yard of pace, he was still canny enough to look after himself in the middle. His exploits for the 'Mean Machine' of Transvaal were well known amongst the squad, so there was no objection to his leadership.

Because the tour was in November, it didn't give us too much time to see what players were in form domestically. We went with the guys we knew had done well over a couple of seasons and, considering the hasty turnaround, I thought we did okay. It doesn't happen too often that a team full of debutants has quite so much experience, but we managed to get stalwarts like Jimmy Cook, Ricey, keeper Dave Richardson, and then the excitement of a young attack that included the really fast Allan Donald, and the swing of Richard Snell.

Adrian Kuiper was one of the hardest hitters of a ball I had ever seen, and he bowled some handy medium pace, too. We ticked a lot of boxes, and we had left-armer Tim Shaw as the spin option. Getting to Calcutta, as it was known then, was an adventure in itself. A lot of us were taken out of our comfort zones. India, as many will tell you, is an attack on all your senses. The minute you land there as a tourist, you are taken aback by the sheer vastness of it all.

What's more, as cricketers, you are immediately elevated to a lot more than just another tourist. It is a country that lives for cricket, and whether you are in the breakfast room, in a cab, at a restaurant or the airport, there will be the obligatory piece of advice from a local. South Africa has always had a mix of sports, different seasons that dictated what was played.

In India, it is cricket. And then more cricket. To be in a place that lived for one sport was quite the start for our team of newbies. But it was more than just the cricket. We certainly had no idea what traffic meant, and the sheer volume of people on the streets, around the hotel, at practice, at the welcome press conference, it was all pretty overwhelming.

But all those people were nothing compared to the 90,000 that crammed into Eden Gardens on 10 November 1991 for our very first one-day international. The rumour was that they were trying to break the world record, but they were not sure if they pulled it off. Whether or not they did, they certainly had more firecrackers in a sporting venue. The smog that greeted Cook and Andrew Hudson when they walked out to bat was incredible. It was very early, a 9am start, but already the stands were absolutely crammed.

We had been told that India truly loved their cricket, but we had no way of being able to comprehend it without seeing it for ourselves. They cheered at the mere sight of their players, and wickets and boundaries were greeted with huge roars. It was, in a sense, an intimidating scene, but we were too busy pinching ourselves about the fact that it was happening. I can still remember Ali, smartly turned out in a suit, clapping on the openers.

How he managed to stop sweating in a full suit, in the cauldron that was Calcutta, was really remarkable, but the pride on his face told quite a story, too. He was immensely proud, and quite justifiably, too. He would later describe it as the greatest day in his life, which was saying a lot. If you consider that Ali had captained (albeit briefly) a team regarded as one of the best on paper for his country, and then all he achieved in his personal capacity, to rank our first day back in the international fold as the best said just how much South African cricket meant to him. This had been a long time coming, and now it was finally happening. I want to say it didn't matter that we got beaten in the first match, but it did. We were a proud team, and were well aware that the world was also looking on with intrigue at what we would bring to the table.

In the circumstances, scoring 177 for 8 was never going to be enough. Kepler Wessels scored a battling half-century, and he got some support from Kuiper, but our top order hadn't fired. India were in early trouble, thanks to Donald's burst with the new ball, but their ship was steadied by a youngster by the name of Sachin Tendulkar.

We had already heard about this teenage sensation, who had made his Test debut when most people were still at school, and on that day he showed what the fuss was about. It wasn't that he blew us away, but rather the fact that he took charge of the situation, and calmly repelled everything that our attack threw at him. He was very correct, very still, and he struck all of us as a star in the making. Quite how big a star he would be was to become apparent as the years rolled on. Tendulkar's fifty, and another by debutant Pravin Amre, saw India home by three wickets. Though it sounds closer on paper, it was a lot more comfortable for the home side.

In the post-match presentation, Ricey illustrated exactly why he was the perfect choice for captain. Asked how it felt to be on the losing side, he noted that he knew what Neil Armstrong had felt like when he walked on the moon. It pretty much summed up the mood in the dressing room. Playing that first game felt like achieving the impossible, but now we wanted to show that we could play as well.

Though the cricket was very important to us, a real highlight of the tour for everyone was the chance to meet one of the world's most respected figures. Mother Teresa was one of those iconic leaders whose example of peace and goodwill resonated globally. We had seen her in pictures from around the world, and we had heard of her remarkable work, but the chance to go and meet her as a squad was overwhelming.

I remember all of us being very aware of the need for protocol. We were hushed, respectful and in awe of the entire experience. As sportsmen and women, there are certain privileges that are handed to you that are beyond words. We knew that there were people in India who would travel thousands of miles, most of them by foot, just to say they saw Mother Teresa. So, to be given the chance to meet her was definitely something we cherished.

If travelling to India had felt like a bit of a spiritual experience, that day fully confirmed it as such. Our trip was about a lot more than cricket, and the friendliness of our hosts showed us just what we had been missing. Another terrific experience for us was the day trip to the Taj Mahal. Again, much like the visit to Mother Teresa, it was something that caught us completely off guard. We had heard the legend of the Taj Mahal, but none of us had figured that we may get the chance to go there on a whirlwind tour.

But, as Ali kept on mentioning, our maiden trip to India was about a lot more than just cricket. When we were told that we would be going to see one of the wonders of the world, it hadn't dawned on us just how far we would have to travel to get there. Bear in mind that the roads in India at that time were not as good as they are now. We went in between the second and third one-day matches, and when we were told that it was a trip of close to 200km, we figured it would be a couple of hours. Of course, it proved to be about double that, as we weaved through the endless traffic.

But, all agreed that it was time very well spent. The trip itself may have been uncomfortable at times, but once you saw the magnificence for the first time, it was awe-inspiring. The sheer size of it is staggering, and then there are the thousands of people who are there on a daily basis. Many apparently come there often, to find peace or to try and rekindle love. You can see why, too, because it is a place of great peace, even amidst the chaos. Once you are inside, it is like a library, and everyone has to leave their shoes outside. There were a few nervous glances from the boys, but touring teaches you to be respectful of customs around the world. We had already been jumped to the front of a very long queue, so we couldn't really complain!

The drive back to Delhi was possibly even longer, but the bus was quiet and reflective for a very long part of the journey. Who knows what was going on in each mind? I do remember thinking that excursions like that, to see Mother Teresa and the Taj Mahal, were massive for team-building, because it reminded us that we were part of a bigger picture. The scenes and sights of India outside of cricket break your heart, because it reminds you just how fortunate you are. Sure, we had problems in South Africa, but a massive part of the population in India was living in conditions that left us speechless. By the time we eventually got to the hotel, we were all exhausted. It had been a long day, but one that would stay with each one of us for a very long time.

Even though we were learning much away from the game, we still hadn't properly acclimatised to the conditions on the field. It was a baptism of fire in that respect, because the conditions were just unlike anything we had played in before. That was in no way an excuse, but we were learning on the job. India was also the first time we had encountered proper reverse swing, and the mystery of how it suddenly came about. Prabhakar and Kapil Dev were almost unplayable at times, and we were baffled as to how they were getting the ball to do so much, when we were just working with conventional swing.

The surfaces in India had a lot to do with it. They were dry and abrasive; perfect for scuffing up one side of the ball, and priming the other side for a touch of reverse swing. As a batsman, you could always prepare for conventional swing. You knew that the new ball would go a certain way, and you made the necessary adjustments. Reverse was a different kettle of fish, though. It made even great batsmen look silly, and the very best exponents could literally make the ball bend around corners. It was humbling, but also something that was annoying, because it felt like an uneven playing field. During the second one-dayer, we got to a point where we felt that there must be some ball-tampering going on, because the bowling suddenly became unplayable.

For that second one-day match, we handed Mandy Yachad and Clive Eksteen their debuts. Mandy came in for Andrew Hudson, who was unlucky, but it was a short tour. Eksteen, a left-arm spinner of some promise, was one we hoped could exploit the dry conditions in Gwalior, venue for the second game of the series.

We needed a good start, but India won the toss and elected to bat first. The match had been reduced to 45 overs, and their opening pair of Kris Srikkanth and Navjot Sidhu looked intent on batting all the overs themselves. It was tough in the heat for our boys, and poor Eksteen was targeted by the well-set pair. That is the problem with cricket sometimes; you can make all the plans in the world, but you never really know what the opposition is going to throw at you out in the middle.

Again, we had Donald to thank for at least slowing things down. Our spearhead came back with three late wickets, and our target was set at 224, nearly five runs to the over. This became an especially tough task when we lost Jimmy Cook in the first over. It was the second time we had lost an opener right away, and it is always hard to bounce back from that.

Kepler's Test experiences with Australia continued to show, as he again led our scoring. His second consecutive half-century came at a much better scoring rate, but he again lacked support. We had come into the second match hoping to square the series, but ended up losing our way completely. We limped to 185 for 8, with their spinner Raju cleaning up the middle order, after our top order had again been blown away. These were tough lessons for us to take, but they were necessary. We still felt strongly enough about the ball that we had instructed our number 11, Allan Donald, to try and get a close look at it when he went out to bat. As an opening bowler, we figured Allan could tell a bit more about these things, and could at least give us a viewpoint. As it played out, he never got to the crease, because the ninth-wicket stand was unbroken!

By the time the final game came around, we had decided to go back to our traditional strengths. The pitch in Delhi looked a good deal firmer, and the weather itself was actually a lot cooler than the other parts of India we had been to. When we were informed at the hotel that Delhi had a genuine winter, we were even more surprised. It turns out you learn new things all the time.

The final match of the series was a day/night affair, which meant we had a hard white ball to bowl with, and an even more partisan crowd to drown out. India had won the toss and elected to bat first, no doubt buoyed by the fact that they had put a lot of pressure on us in Gwalior. What they hadn't reckoned with was the mood in our camp. You couldn't tell that we had lost the series, and everyone wanted to leave the series on a positive note. Before the match, the two captains released doves into the sky, as a symbol of the peace and the friendship between the two countries. It was another nice touch, and no one who went on that trip will ever forget what India did for South African cricket.

We went in without a spinner, backing our pace attack and our all-rounders to see us home. When India pummelled almost 300 off us, it didn't look too clever. Ravi Shastri and Sanjay Manjrekar both hit fine centuries, in a massive partnership for the second wicket. At times, the noise from the stands made it hard to hear what we were saying to each other in the dressing room. I could only imagine what the din was like in the middle. There are a few grounds in the world where it is no fun to be chasing leather from the home side. Australia has a few, and grounds like Headingley and The Oval in England get quite lively. But the wall of noise in India can sometimes feel like it is never-ending. I am sure that they thought the game was over, even before the lights took effect for the second innings. But, they had forgotten about Kepler, who had already notched two fifties. Somehow, he outdid himself again in the last game, with a terrific 90. He deserved a hundred, and even to hit the winning runs, but fell just short.

The key to our success, which was achieved with more than three overs to spare, was a good start. Kepler and Cook added 70-odd for the first wicket, and that foundation allowed Peter Kirsten to come into a situation where India were defending, rather than surrounding him. Our silver fox took centre stage, and struck the kind of knock that showed what the world had been missing. 'Kirsy' always had a lot of time to play his shots, and he was exceptional that night. The flicks off his leg, and his driving off the back foot were top-class, and we noted more than a few ripples of applause from the appreciative crowd.

That knock from Kirsten certainly helped in the debate about him going to the World Cup, once we were told the wonderful news that we were in. That night, in Delhi, he showed that his appetite for the big stage was still as strong as ever, and we would certainly need that x-factor in crunch games. Our win was clinical, and Kepler was rightly judged as joint man of the series with India's Manoj Prabhakar, whose probing spells with the new ball were a real thorn in our side throughout the series.

Though our time in India was brief, it had been incredible. The matches themselves had given us plenty of food for thought, and we could see that there were certain areas that we lacked. There were some quality players on the Indian team then, and they very quickly showed us where we stood in the world pecking order. For a long time, we hadn't had a proper gauge, but the likes of Kapil Dev, Prabhakar and Tendulkar, of course, revealed much to us.

The day-night in Delhi was very good homework for the World Cup, as the combination of a good pitch, the white ball and a capacity crowd gave us a glimpse of what we would have to face in Australia. The fact that we had come out on top was heartening, even if it didn't help in the series. Some may say it was a dead rubber but, in our minds, there was no such thing as a dead rubber, especially in those first few years back in the international fold. Every game was a slice of history, a chance to do what we hadn't done for a long time.

India had been a beautiful blur, and something we could never forget. As I sat on the plane, two things occupied my mind. Thankfully, kit was no longer one of them. We still didn't know if we were going to the World Cup, because the ICC, and key members within the structure, still had reservations about the political landscape in South Africa. Ali and Mr Tshwete still had to prove that we were representing a country now united, and there was a referendum that was pending a nation's approval.

The second thought was a lot more optimistic. If we did go to the World Cup, I was certain that we would surprise a few teams. The rapid emergence of Allan Donald as a strike bowler was exciting. I had a feeling that Warwickshire would have tried to convince him to try and play for England if South Africa hadn't returned to international cricket, so the timing of our comeback was very good for him. Of course, Allan went on to take over 300 wickets in Test cricket, and provided South Africans with some fine memories. He had certainly used his time in the UK to bulk up a lot from the scrawny, wild kid I had seen in Bloemfontein just a few years before.

The other intriguing prospect for me was the form of Peter Kirsten and Kepler Wessels, our two most senior batsmen. Kepler had been toughened up by playing for Australia for a few years, but had wasted little time in availing himself to his country of birth when the door was opened again. He was a fighter – not always the prettiest batsman – but he found a way to score runs. At the other end, Peter was like an old pro. Some of his contemporaries just missed out on even a brief international career, but he at least got a few years to show what he could do.

Besides those two, we also had several players who were unknown, and gaining confidence all the time. Richard Snell's swing bowling was a potent threat, especially if we bowled under lights. I felt he could break a game open, working in tandem with Allan's speed at the other end. We had quite a few all-rounders as well, and they would be a lot more comfortable on Australian pitches, which were not dissimilar to ours. All in all, India had been a perfect opportunity to introduce us to real cricket, way out of the comfort zones we knew, and we were a lot better for it. Certainly, it helped the team spirit, because we had to stick together as one team. No longer could we say we were Natal players, or Western Province players. We were all South African, and the objective was to be the best South African team possible. That was a happy new thought.

The tour, though hastily arranged, had been a success. Even though we lost the series, we had managed to get some invaluable experience on and off the field. I thought the trip had also proved why Ali was the man to lead South African cricket through the waters of transition. There had been some bumping of heads with the Indian board over issues during the course of the trip. Ali had dealt with them swiftly, and though he never appeared out of joint to us, he must have had stressful times. We were still new kids on the block, and it would have been easier to just bend to every demand made of him as the team manager.

As a former international player himself, he was acutely aware of the need for players to be left alone to their thoughts ahead of a game, and he made sure that there were no unnecessary functions the night before a match. Those small touches meant a lot to the coaching staff, and we were chuffed to get at least one win under the belt. We had shown that we had the ability to perform and compete in the first two games, but nothing speaks louder than a win.

The once-in-a-lifetime meeting with Mother Teresa, and the trip to the Taj Mahal, were all particular highlights for us. Mother Teresa is a global icon, and to spend some time in her company had a profound impact on the team. The picture of Ricey standing next to her, his hands together in religious respect, remains one of my favourite memories.

The Taj Mahal, magnificent and grand, was also incredible. Just to try and imagine the hours and hours of painstaking work that had gone into it was mind-blowing. We had never seen anything like it, and it was certainly worth the trek.

The whole trip to India, as sudden as it was, had been worth all the effort. We were back in business.

Chapter 3

1992 World Cup

GOING TO the World Cup in 1992 was never a sure thing for us. Immediately after we had been re-admitted into international cricket, after the annual meeting at Lord's, Ali Bacher had told us that it was too short notice for us to make the cut for the event in Australia. We accepted that, because it was enough for all of us to be back in the international fold.

So we went off to India for the one-dayers, which was an incredible experience. When we got back home, the players got stuck into domestic cricket, and the coaching staff got an opportunity to evaluate what we needed to be competitive in the international arena. There were no trips on the agenda, with everyone building to the World Cup, so we knew we had some time.

It was important to start thinking ahead. A core of our players had enjoyed long careers playing Currie Cup cricket, but the return to the international fold was just at the end of their time. It was a pity, but we had to start thinking about the next few years, instead of the next two matches. I knew that Ali hadn't completely given up the World Cup ghost, but I wasn't too optimistic. It was too tight a turnaround, surely.

As we closed off the year 1991, I breathed a sigh of relief. We were back in international cricket, and I had the privilege of playing some role in the team that was representing a united South Africa. As it turned out, the reason for us being question marks for the World Cup was because a large percentage of the member boards were still not convinced that South Africa was united as a country.

It must have been hard to believe that a team that was still almost exclusively white was representing a nation with a rich diversity of people – with white people being the minority. Those imbalances were still in the process of being acknowledged, and 25 years later, the face of South African cricket has changed to be a lot more representational, happily. Back in 1992, there was still some resistance from some corners that we were being allowed back into the world game without assurances that there was an actual revolution.

We hadn't yet had elections, but the release of Mr Nelson Mandela had said more to the people of the world than any speech could have. Things were changing, and if we had missed the World Cup boat in the process, no one would have felt slighted. Our country was in the midst of something monumental, and that took far greater priority.

So, it was with some surprise that I received Ali's latest phone call of consequence. I wonder how much he actually slept in our first year back. He was always on the phone across the world, confirming this, and explaining that, and doing all he could to get his country back on the map.

'We are in,' he said quietly.

'We are going to the World Cup.'

I took a moment to let that sink in. The World Cup was something that came about after isolation. I remember the first World Cup, in 1975. I had been at Gloucestershire for a few seasons, and things were going well for us on the field, and we had settled into life in Bristol as a family. But that very first World Cup reminded me of what I was missing. Clive Lloyd played one of the great knocks by a captain in a final, the very first World Cup Final, and the West Indies became the first world champions. That Saturday in June was a great day for cricket, and the tournament has gone on to be the global spectacle that it is now.

By 1992, there was coloured clothing, white balls and the drama of playing under lights. It was a thrill, and now Ali was saying that we were going to be a part of it. It was terrific news, but also meant that we had to get our ducks in a row quite quickly. White-ball cricket had been part of our domestic game for almost ten years, with the Benson & Hedges Nite Series. It was great fun, and always enjoyed phenomenal support. I know that the sold-out signs which were hardly seen in domestic cricket nowadays were standard procedure back then. Sure, there were fewer options for the family that wanted to stay at home, but the spectacle of bright colours everywhere – from orange stumps, to all the crazy colours teams wore – under lights, with an endless smell of braai meat was hard to beat. Western Province (WP) had dominated the series for most of the 80s, winning a ridiculous six titles in a row. Eastern Province (EP) were always competitive, while Transvaal had experience and some great batting up front. Natal were a young team on the rise, and Free State had some terrific pros, as well as a young Allan Donald, who would wear zinc war-paint on his face, and must have been a terrifying prospect on a hard wicket, under lights, and with a full house baying for a bouncer.

So we were not going to get caught cold by the playing conditions. What would come as a surprise to some, I thought, may be the quality that we came up against. We had been put under real pressure by the skill of India's pacemen with the white ball in the final match in New Delhi, so we knew that other teams would also have a great skill-set. Ali wanted me to be a part of the selection panel, given that I was going to be the coach. The only issue with that was he hadn't reckoned with the politics within South African cricket. The chairman of selectors was Peter van der Merwe, who was an EP man through and through. Peter had played for South Africa and captained the first South African side to beat Australia in a Test series, in 1966/67.

The president of South African cricket was Geoff Dakin, who I thought was one of the best administrators in world cricket – and played a major role in uniting South African cricket – was also from Port Elizabeth. With both men being from the same part of the world, it meant that they were naturally quite close to Kepler Wessels. Between the two of them, they had an idea of what kind of team we should take to Australia. Kepler had played there, and even earned a baggy green, so he knew what he was talking about. I still felt quite strongly that we could take the experienced players that had been in India, and then look to build beyond the World Cup.

I really wanted Clive Rice and Jimmy Cook to come to the World Cup, alongside Peter Kirsten. Clive was still bowling very well, and Jimmy and 'Kirsy' had very good hands, worth a few catches in a tournament. Those were my most pressing thoughts, and I tried to raise them at the first meeting we had as a selection panel. By virtue of being captain, Kepler was also a part of that discussion. Try as I might, I couldn't get them to back all three of our senior batsmen. They had it in their minds to move forward, and they didn't want to take Clive and Jimmy with them. They said Peter Kirsten was an option, but the entire matter was very strained. I felt like a visitor, and told Ali I didn't see the point of me travelling all the way to Port Elizabeth for meetings when things were already decided.

When the preliminary squad was announced, there was an outcry. How could we possibly go to the biggest tournament of our lives without three of our best batsmen even in the preliminary squad that still had to be trimmed down to 15 players? Kirsten had already shown in India that he was seeing the ball pretty well, while Clive and Jimmy's class was undisputed. The simple truth of it was that there was always going to be a tussle when it came to picking a national team after so many years of not doing so. Sanity eventually prevailed when Kirsten did end up going to the World Cup, and his performances there probably raised the question of how far we would have gone if we had the other 'wise heads' with us.

Another bone of contention was that of Jonty Rhodes. I knew him well from a young age, having coached him a bit when he was a schoolboy showing terrific progress in Pietermaritzburg. It sounds convenient now, of course, but there was always a feeling that Jonty was worth having in the field for that bit of magic he could provide. Jonty's hockey pedigree meant he was phenomenal against spin. His hands allowed him to manufacture shots, and he never ever seemed to get done for length by spin. But I also felt Jonty's role in the field couldn't be overstated. I even went as far as saying that I thought we were looking at one of the world's best fielders at a press conference in the lead-up to the tournament. I don't think too many people took it seriously.

The World Cup looked like it was going to be a tournament played on hard, fast surfaces. That meant our bowlers would likely go back of a length, and with the leg-side wide rule, you were more than likely to hit a lot of balls square, or just behind square on the off side. By the time he had finished striding in, Jonty was usually 15 yards from the bat, and his anticipation saved us a pile of runs. Good shots got no reward, and batsmen would sometimes get out trying to hit the ball a little finer, in order to avoid him. Trying to take quick singles to his area was also hazardous, and he was unwittingly playing a starring role in revolutionising fielding in the modern game.

He was a modern reminder that South Africa's renowned fielding standards still held firm. The tour of 1952/53 to

Australia, captained by Jackie Cheetam, had earned South Africa a formidable reputation in the field. Russell Endean was probably the star fielder in the team, but a number of the other players also had moments of brilliance in the Test series. South Africa had realised that, on paper, they were significantly inferior to an Australian side boasting such names as Neil Harvey, Lindsay Hassett, Arthur Morris, Keith Miller and Ray Lindwall, to name but a few. By all accounts, South Africa, with their modest attack, highlighted fielding as being of paramount importance. Against all odds, they drew the five-match Test series 2-2, famously winning the fifth Test at Melbourne by four wickets, chasing 297.

Much of the foundation for that series had been in their fielding, and it played a mighty role in sharing the series. Ten years later, Colin Bland continued that fine tradition with his astonishing fielding abilities, and he was regarded as dangerous back then as Rhodes was in the 90s. With Jonty in the side, the standard of our fielding rose a few notches in intensity, even at practice. He was a good man to have in the squad, and he was to become another fielding sensation from South Africa to leave his mark on Australian soil.

So, even though we were in the tournament, we still had an uphill struggle to settle on a squad to take there. I was quite happy, in the end. Our attack had some very good swing bowlers. Guys like Meyrick Pringle and Richard Snell were always going to be a handful with a white ball, and under lights. Again, we felt that the World Cup was another chance for us to spring a few surprises. The trip to India had taught us that we needed to be a bit more positive up front, and that spin could definitely be used as a strength, which was a mindset we were still getting accustomed to. India had also shown us that we had the talent, and the likes of Allan Donald, Kepler and, of course, Peter Kirsten, would be real trump cards for us. There was also the unknown all-round ability of the powerful Adrian Kuiper, a man who could destroy an attack on his day.

In the background, Ali was still working frenetically to appease any concerns around the legitimacy of the team we were bringing. There was to be a nationwide poll in South Africa, in the middle of the tournament, which would assess if the whole country was behind a change of rule. Ali, minister of sport Steve Tshwete and the ANC convinced the ICC that the vote would be unanimous, and they granted us our place in the World Cup on good faith.

Everyone knew who Ali Bacher was, but our minister of sport, the late Steve Tshwete, was an unsung hero. His passion and positivity towards us had a great impact on the team, because they knew that people back home were behind us. Steve was a wonderful man, and a very keen follower of sport. He lived every ball with us during that opening match against Australia and, when we won, his spontaneous peck of Peter Kirsten's bald head summed him what he meant to us as a team perfectly. He was a great man for the country, and he certainly batted for us throughout that frenetic World Cup period, allowing us to concentrate fully on playing the game.

Someone else who was an unsung hero and played a significant role in our run to the semi-final was Allan Jordaan, the team manager. Allan was an attorney by trade, and was a great sportsman in his own right. He had captained North Eastern Transvaal in his playing days, and was later one of the key players in the unification of cricket in South Africa. At the World Cup, he kept the players happy, and was a great sounding board for the players, able to give them confidence ahead of the big challenges. He also shared his extensive cricketing knowledge when it was asked for, and was a popular man in the team.

Incredible as it may sound, if the vote had inexplicably gone the other way, we would have been booted out of the tournament, regardless of what point we were at. It wasn't really the kind of thing you wanted to think about too much, especially when we found out our first match was against the hosts. But, it was there in the back of the minds of the management team, for sure. For the players, though, it was another opportunity to test their mettle. We didn't leave South Africa with the idea of becoming world champions, but we were certain that we could compete. We had a great responsibility, as we were one of the very first teams to represent the new South Africa at a major, global competition, and there were more than a few glistening eyes when we were received as warmly as we were in Sydney. In a matter of eight months, we had gone from envious spectators to full-on participants, and we just couldn't wait to get stuck in.

Personally, it was good to be back in Australia, though a lot had changed in the decade since. For one thing, I was going to have a look at the proper stadiums this time, instead of the ground-breaking venues that hosted our World Series contests. For another, all of Australia was enthralled by the World Cup. They love their sport, and they were already giving us a good ribbing ahead of the first game, certain that we would struggle to step up under the glare of the cricket world.

But we were quietly confident, especially after New Zealand beat Australia in the opening game of the tournament. We knew that they would have their backs against the wall, while we were the newcomers, with no pressure on us at all. We had drummed in the importance of starting with intent, and giving ourselves a chance to do something special. Our series in India had been characterised by bad starts, which left too much to do at the back end. Now, having learnt from those experiences, we were keen to make an immediate impression. In the background, Ali and the minister of sport were still chipping away, ensuring that our continued participation was on the right track. As a team, though, we were only focussed on making a strong start in Sydney. At the best of times, the SCG is a cracking place to be for a cricket match. But, in the circumstances, 26 February 1992 was even more special.

We couldn't have hoped for a better start – or so we thought. Australia won the toss and decided to bat first. That was fine by us, because we preferred to start out on the field, as a team. Then Donald produced *that* ball to Geoff Marsh. To this day, everyone who was behind the bat swears they heard the nick, loud and clear. Allan was already celebrating, but he turned around to find umpire Brian Aldridge unmoved. An injustice like that can sometimes push a bowler or a team to try too hard, but Allan was a picture of concentration. He just glided in, and kept on hitting an irresistible length. He had shown us a glimpse of his ability to handle pressure in India, and now he was doing it again, with the world watching.

At the other end, Richard Snell was also making himself known, troubling the experienced David Boon with his swing and bounce. We soon had Boon run out, thanks to fine work by Snell and Hansie Cronje, prowling in the covers. We had said amongst ourselves that our fielding was worth a wicket in itself, and we had just proved it. Between Hansie and Jonty, our cover region was fraught with danger for batsmen, and our bowlers were no slouches in the outfield, either. Allan had one of the slickest arms in the game, and Snell could surprise you with his sling, too. He was one of the unsung heroes that day, with his nine overs going for just 15 runs, and ensuring that the pressure was always on.

We also had a stack of all-rounders in our team, with Hansie, Adrian Kuiper and Brian McMillan all capable of chipping in to swing a match with a wicket, or a crucial knock. Kuiper stood up that day in Sydney, with the scalps of Marsh and Allan Border first up, to really put the cat amongst the pigeons. We had the Aussies on the run, and another of our all-rounders, big Brian McMillan, also got in on the act. By the time Allan Donald came back for the last rites, we had throttled them to 179, with the match reduced by one over each. We fancied chasing down 170, but even we were surprised by how clinical it was.

There was no pressure in terms of run-rate, and that suited Kepler down to the ground. He simply dug in as opener, and made sure he was there to the end. His opening stand with Hudders relaxed the changing room, and Peter Kirsten then calmly took us over the line with 13 balls to spare. It was all a bit of a dream. We had just trounced one of the supposed favourites, in their backyard, and we had barely broken a sweat. We toasted the victory and the occasion with a few beers, but we knew that there was still a lot of work that lay ahead. Far from becoming cocky, we saw the Aussie defeat as a lesson to not take anything for granted. We were pumped, but we were sent crashing down to earth three days later.

This time, Kirsy's 90 was in vain, as he got very little support from the rest of the batters. New Zealand surprised us by opening the bowling with spinner Dipak Patel, and he got Hudders early. We never really got going, and despite Kirsten's second contribution of note, 190 was never enough on Eden Park. The Kiwi openers Mark Greatbatch and Rod Latham then showed us how we could have played, and their century stand meant that the great Martin Crowe was barely needed. It was a good wake-up call, and we knew we had come up desperately short. Our bowling lengths had been wrong on that wicket, and we hadn't got going with the bat. But the nature of a World Cup, especially in those days, doesn't allow one to wallow for too long, and we soon had Sri Lanka in our sights, in Wellington. We didn't know too much about the island just below India, except for the fact that they had some very good spinners, and their middle order of Arjuna Ranatunga and Aravinda de Silva was very classy. To our horror, Ranatunga also decided to chance his golden arm that day, and helped himself to two wickets. 195 all out gave us half a shout, especially with the wicket taking some turn. We had opted for Omar Henry, and he didn't let us down. He controlled his flight and pace beautifully, and seemed to relish the chance to go up against quality players of spin. Sadly, we just didn't have enough runs, and Ranatunga's rollicking fifty, which was undefeated, saw his men home.

Suddenly, the win over Australia seemed a very distant memory, and we were in danger of falling out of the competition altogether. The last thing we wanted was to be one-hit wonders, beating mighty Australia and then caving under the weight of expectation. When we faced the West Indies, it felt like a knockout game, and it had an edge to it. The press played up the battle, and we were just as excited about the prospect of facing the might of the island nation for the first time ever. They were a team full of pace and stars, and we knew that we were up against it.

They were expected to beat us, given the talent in their ranks. But, thanks to another half-century from Kirsten and contributions from Rhodes, Kuiper, McMillan and Richardson, we managed to just get to 200. We were still not blowing sides away with the bat, but we had given ourselves a chance, so long as the Windies top order didn't fire. As it happened, they ran into one of the most savage spells of swing bowling in the tournament. Meyrick Pringle had enjoyed an excellent season domestically, and now he showed one of the world's most cavalier sides what he could do, with a return of 8-4-11-4. Jonty held on to a sharp chance from Brian Lara at point for Meyrick's first wicket, but then his swing did the rest. Snell again stood up with 2-16 in seven miserly overs. Only Gus Logie hung about for the Windies, as we rolled them for 136, and got our campaign back on track. Some of the press had joked that Meyrick, with his mop of hair, looked like a member of a rock band, and he certainly played like a rock star that day. He took that catch to get rid of Logie, and we knew we were home then.

Next up was Pakistan, at the Gabba. We were certainly seeing a lot of Australasia, though the tight schedule didn't leave too much room for sight-seeing. Of course, once you have a win again, things always look a little brighter. We knew that the Gabba was a big ground, and a good surface to bat on. We were up against a team that had some terrific exponents of swing and reverse swing, so batting first would be handy. There was also some bad weather about, so we were surprised when Imran Khan decided to bowl first. Perhaps it was the overhead conditions, but we thought it would make more sense to put runs on the board first.

As it was, we were without our talisman Peter Kirsten, due to a hamstring strain. Hudders did make a welcome return to form, though, with a fluent half-century. Mark Rushmere also looked good, until he was undone by the leggie, Mushtaq Ahmed. Hansie had been quiet with the bat, but he was renowned as an aggressive player of spin, so we had kept him in the side to look after Mushtaq. Hansie made a fine 47 not out, and he confirmed his billing as one of our better players against spin. He was a big man, which meant he could stride down the wicket, but he also had a very good eye. He seemed to pick Mushtaq right away, and he hit him for several clean boundaries. But, we didn't have things all our own way. Wasim Akram had been unsuccessful with the new ball, but he came back later with the reversing ball, and castled Brian McMillan when he was well set to finish strongly. Dave Richardson fell in the same fashion, and we ended on only just over 200.

The weather that had concerned us was now a real factor. With Pakistan going along very nicely, on 70-odd for 2, we went off for an hour due to rain. We hadn't been exposed to the rain permutations before that, but we were surprised to learn that their target was now 194 from 36 overs. It meant that they suddenly had to motor, having set themselves up for a well-paced chase. But, those were the rules, and we resumed play. The match will always be remembered for what happened soon after that resumption, when Imran Khan and Inzamam-ul-Haq dithered over a quick single. The ball was just behind square, in the Jonty zone, and ul-Haq was going to the danger end. He must have figured Jonty would have a shy, but our star fielder backed himself in the foot race, and flung himself into back pages and front pages around the world. The grainy image of him, horizontal, ball in hand, and running out one of the world's most destructive batsmen, remains one of the best moments in World Cup history. In the context of the match, it stopped a rampant Inzamam from really getting stuck in. He had obviously been given licence to attack, and he had started to play his full range of strokes. Jonty stopped him dead in his tracks, and Pakistan themselves never recovered from the shock. They ultimately fell 20 runs short, but we knew that we had got away with one. It was later worked out that if the Duckworth/Lewis method had been used, their revised target after the rain delay would have been 162 instead of 194. That would have seen them beat us with an over to spare, so we knew we had got the rub of the green. With the very strict TV times, the playing conditions were really tilted to the team batting first, because they at least couldn't be hit too hard by the calculations. We sat and hoped that we wouldn't fall victim to what had happened to Pakistan.

Our trek across Australia took us to the Manuka Oval next to meet a familiar foe in Zimbabwe. A lot of us had played in Zimbabwe at some point, and we had also had a couple of warm-up matches with them before getting on the plane to the World Cup. So, we were confident of getting the right result. Peter Kirsten made his return to the side, and duly announced himself by burgling three wickets out of nowhere! The Zimbabweans must have felt as bad as we did when we allowed Ranatunga to steal a couple of our scalps, but that is the nature of cricket. Once Kirsten had laid claim to the title of all-rounder with the ball, he and Kepler were clinical in our chase of 164. Kepler got out before the end, for 70, but Kirsten was there, not out on 62. He was enjoying an unbelievable World Cup, and it was scary to think where we would have been if he had been ousted, along with the very unlucky Jimmy Cook and Clive Rice.

We were looking good for the semi-finals, but we needed at least one more win to make that a done deal. England at the mighty MCG was next, which was a fixture we had all circled when we first saw the draw. England were the old enemy, and it was fitting that we met them on such a grand stage. The match lived up to expectation, too, with lots of runs, some wonderful individual performances, and a bit of drama at the end.

We thought we were in the pound seats after batting first, and getting off to a cracking start. Kirsten had a quiet match, for once, but Kepler and Hudders had already spanked 151 for the opening partnership. Finally, we had the start we dreamt of, even if it was a touch slow towards the end. The middle order couldn't quite get going after that, unfortunately, and what could have been 270 and out of sight, ended up being 236 for 4. It was a decent total, but England knew they had been let off the hook somewhat.

In reply, their keeper/batsman Alec Stewart batted like a dream up front. Scoring at almost a run a ball, he gave them the early impetus, and we got caught up trying to get him out with the short ball, instead of sticking to our channels. When we got Ian Botham, Graeme Hick and Robin Smith out for the addition of one run, we really fancied our chances, especially as it came after a rain delay that had seen their target altered to 226 from 41 overs. Considering that they were already on 62 from 12 overs, it was another strange recalculation, because it brought us back into the game.

Stewart found a buddy in Neil Fairbrother, one of the game's great chasers in one-day cricket. The pair of them kept the rate rattling along, and they also ran very well between the wickets –

well, until Stewart took on Jonty and came up short. Again, it was on a knife edge, but England knew that Fairbrother was the key. Chris Lewis played a good hand, but he was also run out by Jonty, who was still surprising batsmen, even after the Inzamam affair. We kept on nicking wickets but Fairbrother kept up with the rate, and we eventually succumbed in the final over, with just one ball to spare. It was a wonderful match, worthy of a final, perhaps, but we were left to rue our missed chances – especially with the bat.

Our final group match was against our good friends from India, in Adelaide. We knew we had to win, but rain delayed the start by over three hours. That saw the match reduced to 30 overs a side, and we decided to bowl first, to try and exploit the moist conditions in the air. Allan Donald, who had been quiet for a few matches, struck with the fifth ball of the match, and returned later to oust an ominous-looking Kapil Dev. The thorn in our side that day, though, was Mohammad Azharuddin and his rubber wrists. You just couldn't bowl at the stumps to him, otherwise the ball was flicked away to leg, even from outside off stump sometimes. His 79 saw India to a very competitive 180 in 30 overs, and we knew that we had to play very well to get home. But, Azharuddin's innings had also shown us that the wicket was still a very good one to bat on, despite the rain. With that in the back of our minds, we set about getting into the World Cup semi-finals, at the first attempt.

We had decided to shuffle our batting order, and Kepler had put himself in the middle order. Hudders was to open with Kirsten, who was in some of the best form of his life. We needed a fast start, and they gave us exactly that. We all remembered Kirsten's knock in Delhi, when we had last played India, and he clearly felt like he was still batting on the same deck. He was imperious, and not even the great Kapil Dev could bowl to him. He also cut loose on the left-arm spin of Raju, not allowing him to settle. Hudders sensibly farmed the strike to him, and their massive stand for the first wicket sucked out all the drama from the chase. Even though they both fell before the finish line, they had won us the game, and sent us to the semi-final. We were in dreamland.

Behind the scenes, there was a bit of a storm brewing, which could have ended our World Cup dream in the worst possible way. The proviso for us playing in the tournament was that we had to give assurances that we were representing a country that was united, and that we were going to change government. Mr Nelson Mandela had been released from jail, but we were yet to have our elections, so a lot of what needed to be done was still in the air. There was a national referendum to see if the majority of the population were behind a new government. The results of that vote would confirm whether or not the country we represented was singing from the same song sheet. We were confident that sanity would prevail, but there were still some nervous moments as we waited for the results. They would come out on the eve of the semi-final, and we were due to renew our rivalry with England, this time at the SCG.

I can only shudder at the thought of what would have happened if that referendum had gone the other way. The entire tournament would have been thrown upside down, and we would have been cast as outsiders in the world game once more. Thankfully, the vote was unanimous, and the ICC were finally convinced that change was afoot. We could finally look to the tussle against England, and look to right the wrongs of Melbourne. We had no idea that we were about to play a starring role in one of the craziest finishes to a cricket match, ever.

Rain had already delayed the start by ten minutes, after we had won the toss and elected to field. Again, we felt that our swing bowlers could exploit the overhead conditions, and maybe put England on the back foot. Donald got Graham Gooch to nick off early in the piece, and Pringle castled Ian Botham, to give us the early impetus. Graeme Hick then played one of the better knocks I ever saw from him. He was sometimes accused of being a flat-track bully, and not delivering enough for England. On that day, though, we were on the wrong side of one of his more accomplished knocks. He took the fight to our quicks, and set England on their way to an imposing total. Fairbrother and Alec Stewart chipped in, and their 252 for 6 would have been greater, had their innings not been cut short due to the slow over-rate. They only faced 45 overs, because that was all we could bowl in the allotted time. The game has moved on in many ways since then, and something like cutting the first innings five overs short, due to strict broadcast times, is unheard of these days. Captains are under pressure to finish in the allotted time, but it should never affect the team batting first. Kepler took a lot of flak for our over-rate, because it was his responsibility as captain.

We were docked five batting overs, too, which meant our target was 253 to win from 45 overs. It was a stiff task, but it was a wonderful batting deck. Our primary concern was the weather, because we knew it was still hovering. We had seen what it had done to Pakistan, and we had to try and be ahead of the run-rate, if possible. It was a real pity that we lost our key men, Kepler and Peter, cheaply, because their presence would have been crucial during the tense moments later on in the chase. Kepler's tough day at the office also saw him employed as a runner for Peter. While England had Hick's 83 to work around, we went about the chase by chipping away at it with smaller contributions by most of our batters. Andrew Hudson's 46 up front was well-paced, and Jonty's 43 in the latter stages gave us a sniff. Adrian Kuiper looked like he had saved his hitting for the biggest match of our tournament, but he was outfoxed by the spin of Richard. We knew that we just needed one guy to bat through, and we had enough depth to maybe get over the line. But, England were encouraged by the fact that they kept on getting wickets, and the required rate was climbing all the time.

By the time Dave Richardson had joined big McMillan in the middle, we were needing more than eight runs an over. It wasn't impossible, but we were the underdogs. And then, fatefully, the heavens opened. We knew that with all the earlier delays, and the very strict TV times, we were on a slippery slope. When we went off, we needed 22 runs off 13 balls. The ball was wet, and both our batters were set. Anything could have happened, we figured, as long as we faced out our overs. When the recalculation was announced, we knew it was just about over. 22 off seven, it said. Then, more rain. The final equation on the big screen was 22 off one ball, which was actually wrong. We needed 21 off one ball, not that it would have made a difference. Chris Lewis bowled the final ball, with boos ringing all around the stadium, and a stunned silence in our dressing room.

We were not stunned because we were out of the tournament, not at all. We were just gutted that we hadn't had the chance to see it through to the final ball. Cricket is a funny game, and we knew that anything could happen under that pressure. Looking around the dressing room, there were a few tears, but also a genuine sense of pride in our extraordinary journey. I walked into the South African changing room in 1999, after *that* other semi-final. Now that was a tough place to be, because that South African team were favourites, and the manner of the conclusion was just too incredible for words. In 1992, we were last-minute additions, and we had enjoyed the craziest ride, from the high of beating Australia first up, to the depths of simply running out of time and luck in the semi-final.

We were gutted, of course, because we had all started to believe in the fairy tale. The lap around the ground made us all feel a little better, because it confirmed to us that we had been fully accepted back into the community. We were cheered like champions, by a crowd sympathetic to our circumstances. It was almost unimaginable that a year ago, we had all been resigned to the fact that we would be spectators of the World Cup, with no idea when we would ever get back to the fold. Now, here we were, playing a central role, even if it wasn't the ending that we craved. Some say that started the curse of South Africa in World Cups, but I beg to differ. As a new, emotionally charged side, we had put up a terrific fight, and got a lot further than most expected. We had made our country proud, and also made the cricket world well aware of the talent that we had to show. When one looks back at that World Cup, over 20 years later, it is simply mind-boggling to think that it is still the furthest we have gone at the World Cup as a nation. The 1999 and 2015 World Cups were also semi-finals, of course, but 1992 could have been so different under modern rules.

We had arrived in Australia wide-eyed, but we left with our chests bursting. It had been a hell of a summer, and a hell of a World Cup.

Chapter 4

A Caribbean whistle-stop

OUR MAIDEN tour of the West Indies was one that very nearly didn't happen. For one thing, it was at the end of the most demanding season of our lives, coming after the 1992 World Cup, and the historic tour to India at the end of 1991.

It was the end of a whirlwind period for South African cricket, when everything seemed to be happening at once, after years of isolation. After the World Cup and the reaction to the way we had been ousted in the rain-hit semi against England, there was one last hurdle to overcome before we could go home and take stock.

Significantly, we hadn't yet played a Test match since our return to international cricket, so that was always going to provide extra motivation for the team. In the end, of course, we very nearly won that Test match, only for the fearsome West Indian pace attack to come to the fore.

Long before that final day in Bridgetown, though, even before we set foot on the islands, things didn't look like they would work out. Ali had noted that the West Indians were still lukewarm about our return to the international community. They had abstained from voting when it came to deciding our fate for the World Cup in Australia, and Ali and Steve Tshwete were keen to build bridges with what was a powerhouse in the game.

From the West Indian side, you could understand the reservation to engage with us. Our return had been sudden, and the uniting of South Africa was still a project that was under construction. They needed convincing that it was actually happening, and that is where Ali and our minister of sport and recreation came into their own.

Who better to provide the reassurance than the president-elect, Mr Nelson Mandela himself. Whatever was in the letter that Mandela wrote to the West Indies Cricket Board did the trick. It convinced them that our team had the full support of all South African people, and that things were changing back home. That letter softened the West Indian stance, and a tour comprising three one-day internationals and then a one-off Test was conjured up.

As a new opponent on the scene, and given our history, we were still a novelty to play against. Everywhere we went was a chance to build ties and then look ahead to a future working together. Those initial days were not straightforward, because our touring was serving more than just one purpose. We had to be out there, promoting ourselves, almost re-introducing ourselves as a cricket nation again.

And the players were fantastic ambassadors, too. At the World Cup, several of them had made a name for themselves, so they were no longer anonymous on the streets. Jonty Rhodes's dive to get rid of Inzamam-ul-Haq was still on everyone's lips, and his every move at practice was watched with great interest by the youngsters. They wanted to see what this little man with springs on his feet did to become so good. In that sense, Jonty really played a role in making fielding cool. He wasn't alone, obviously, but that image of him flattening the stumps was a terrific advert for athleticism within the game.

The game was evolving all the time, and becoming more and more athletic. We had seen some fantastic natural fielders in our time, such as Colin Bland, who was lightning in the covers. Jonty, in his own way, elevated that, with his aggressive walking in, his alertness, and his lightning fast reactions to anything within a few metres of him in the point area.

For the kids that came to see him, practices were a treat, because he did exactly what he would do in a match. He anticipated so well, which is something all the best fielders do. They just have a sense of where the ball is going, and they are there to effect a catch or stop a run. He was a terrific nuisance for us to have on the field, because the opposition started to think twice when the ball went towards him. After the Inzamam run-out, teams became even more wary of taking him on, because they knew that he could strike at any time.

But, it wasn't as if the West Indies didn't have their own danger-men on the field. Keith Arthurton was a menace in the same region, with a bullet of a left arm. Brian Lara, their gifted young left-hander was also nippy, while they had a very good slip cordon. They needed to be very good, because their pace battery gave them plenty of chances. We were met by the leaders of the next generation of West Indian fast bowlers, Courtney Walsh and Curtly Ambrose. The two 'Big C's were a formidable double act, capable of squeezing the life out of run-scoring, and also of running through a batting card like a hot knife.

In the one-day series, they also found great support from Anderson Cummins, a young fast bowler from Barbados. The one thing I had always known about the West Indies is that they always had tall, fast bowlers. As long as I had known of the West Indies, as long as I had played against their players in county cricket or during the World Series, they always had lanky, fast men in their line-up. And, wherever we went around the Caribbean on that tour, there would be little boys playing their games of pretend cricket, each one trying to bowl faster than the other.

The pitches in the West Indies also encouraged them to be aggressive. They were firm, hard surfaces, with good bounce for their tall men to utilise. The middle was definitely an intimidating place to be for a batsman, with a massive cordon behind you, and a fast bowler steaming in. And when he tired, he would chuck the ball to another one, just as fast, and just as mean. It was proper, hard cricket, and the fans in the stands also contributed to the air of intimidation. The crowds in the Caribbean were certainly not shy to give their opinions on matters on and off the field, and going about your daily business without receiving some piece of advice was impossible.

Being there in that environment made me understand why guys like Gary Sobers and Viv Richards played with the swagger they did. It was part of the cricketing culture, a form of expression, using bats and balls, instead of words. And the tone varied from island to island, as we discovered. We had always told ourselves that South African cricket was very clan-like, with Western Province keeping to themselves, and Eastern Province, and Natal and every other province fiercely protective of its own identity. But that was nothing compared to the regionalism we saw in the West Indies. They were several nations, strung together to create one team. But each nation had misgivings about any number of players that were not their own.

It got especially peculiar when the people of Barbados threatened to boycott the Test match, because Cummins had been left out, even after his exploits against us in the one-day matches. I had heard of people being unhappy with a selection, of course, but to the point where they would stay away from a match in order to make their feelings crystal clear? It was definitely one way of emphasising a point. They would rather listen to it on the radio instead. That was how seriously West Indians took their cricket and their national pride, and I had always thought that captaining them or coaching them might be one of the harder gigs in cricket. Whatever decision you make, you are certain to annoy somebody, so you simply have to go with your instincts.

It made even more sense that men of the stature of Sobers and Clive Lloyd were revered as leaders of men, because they found a way to unite all the islands behind them and their side when they were captains. Richie Richardson, the captain during our visit, was another flamboyant leader, his manner characterised by his big umbrella hat. Whether he was in the field or batting, it was on his head. Despite his standing, Richardson was still booed throughout the first match, which we found rather strange. It turned out the Jamaican fans were unhappy that the World Cup side had omitted Jeffrey Dujon, one of their own!

The first one-day match was scheduled for Sabina Park, in Jamaica. There was a large, expectant crowd. We felt confident enough going in. Though it had been a long season, quite a few of our batsmen were in good touch, and the fast pitches meant quick run-scoring. During the course of the World Cup, we had got used to chasing, and we felt comfortable continuing in the same vein against the Windies. Unfortunately, we ran into a hurricane that day. Phil Simmons, batting at three, smashed one of the more brutal hundreds we had seen. He and Lara put on a good partnership for the second wicket, but it was the manner of the runs, not the amount, that really stung us. They took advantage of the short, straight boundaries, hitting us off our lengths. There was one shot by Simmons, off debutant Corrie Van Zyl, which disappeared over cover – for six! He then hit Omar Henry over his head, and out the ground. We were later told that someone had stolen the ball, but the police had then retrieved it from them.

We had inadvertently given them the initiative by fielding instead of batting, and the home side never looked back. In the dressing room, we thought we actually did quite well to restrict them to just 287 in the circumstances. The way Simmons was going, they looked like they would go well beyond 300, but we brought it back in the second half of the innings. Chasing 288, in front of a buzzing home crowd, was never going to be easy. As it happened, we never even got close, as we crawled to just 180. Ambrose and Patrick Patterson had given us absolutely nothing in the first ten overs, and the run-out of Kepler certainly didn't help.

We were being throttled, with barely a half-volley to release the pressure. Hudson toiled away to a half-century, and Hansie looked promising in getting to 47, but they just had no support. Hansie and Jonty both got bowled by Cummins, and the extra pace was definitely proving troublesome. If we hadn't already known it, we knew we were in for a real baptism of fire from the quick men, and we had to have better plans. That day, Ambrose didn't get amongst the wickets, but he was as menacing as ever. We never saw a half-volley and, while he created pressure at one end, the likes of Patterson and Cummins attacked at the other.

As a former fast bowler myself, I could only admire the systematic manner in which they dismantled us, but as a coach I knew that we had to make them change a few things, try and force them to play the way we wanted to. That was easier said than done, of course, because Ambrose certainly went according to his own tune. We licked our wounds, and put the 107-run defeat down to a really bad day at the office. Simmons had knocked the stuffing out of us, and there really had been no way back after that.

The second one-dayer moved us to Trinidad, in Port-of-Spain. The crowd swelled, because they were obviously smelling blood. We trained with the same intensity, but we just couldn't really get going. I again remembered Kepler's words about us not rushing into things, and maybe get the players away from the game for a while. But, this was no time for hindsight. We had a series to try and get back into, and we needed to be at our best to do so.

The Windies came hard at us in that game. As we wilted in the heat, they seemed to rise up even more impressively. We had spoken about the need to be positive, with bat and ball, but also with our fielding and our running between the wickets. We had lost two wickets to run-outs in Jamaica, which was unlike us. We were usually good judges of singles, and I could only put it down to mental fatigue. So what then occurred in the game had us all pulling our hair out in the dressing room. Hudson took on backward point, and lost. Kepler and Peter Kirsten, our two bankers, then both fell chasing wide balls. We were already deep in it, but worse was to follow when our two fastest players between the wickets, Hansie and Jonty, both got run out trying to force the issue. We didn't even give ourselves a fighting chance.

As a coach, I could handle losing a match, because it was part of the game. But how you lost said a lot about where you were at as a team, and getting rolled over for just 152 was probably the worst effort I had seen from us since re-admission. It was meek, and tired. It was very concerning, considering that this wasn't even the business end of the tour. We had to hope to hit back with the ball, but there was no relenting from our hosts. Lara was on home turf, and he knew the locals had come in to see him bat. The showman didn't disappoint, either, lashing us all over Sabina Park in an undefeated opening stand of 154 with Desmond Haynes, who also made a half-century.

It was brutal, and our changing room after the match was at the lowest it had been, perhaps all season. The manner of defeat really hurt, and it sounded even worse when it was repeated. Ten wickets, with half the overs still left. That wasn't the team we knew we had, not the team that had made the World Cup semi-finals, and not the team that had gone and won hearts in India, if not the series. This wasn't the team that had waited and waited, for years, to get back on this stage. It was a grim day, and the sooner we got back on to the park, the better it would be for all of us.

So, we moved on to the last game, back at the same venue. Again we were met by a big crowd, who had come to see the West Indians complete the clean sweep. We obviously wanted to win at least one match, and put in a confidence-boosting display before the Test, which was the main event. If we could somehow do what we had done in India, winning the final match of that series, we would at least have some momentum. But, it wasn't Delhi, and it wasn't a belter of a wicket where we could throw caution to the wind.

The Windies were now employing just five bowlers, each bowling their full quota. Richie Richardson had his team operating with precision, and we were trying desperately to keep up. What had become apparent to us during the World Cup was that our scoring at the start of the innings was still a bit laboured. A lot of the other sides were happy to risk losing one wicket, knowing that if their positive batsman came off, they would be off to a rollicking start. We hadn't got that role defined in our team just yet, so we played on as normal. We looked to start solidly – a tough enough task with Ambrose in the form he was in – and then look for the likes of Kuiper to try and cash in towards the end of the innings.

That was the plan, but again it didn't work out that way. It was frustrating that we were getting starts with the bat, and then not capitalising. They always say the hardest thing to do as a batsman is to get to 20. Once you were there, however, you owed it to your team to build something meaningful. Our top four batsmen all got beyond 20 in that last one-dayer, but not one went beyond 45, which meant we never took control of the game as we wanted to. We battled to 189 for 6, but we knew that it wasn't a total that would scare the cock-a-hoop Windies. We needed to bowl especially well, or hope that it was their top-six's turn to have an off day. When Meyrick Pringle bowled Desmond Haynes first up, we had hope. But Phil Simmons then strolled to the crease like a cowboy, and put our hopes to rest. Having already made a century in the first game, he saw fit to repeat the dose in the third match, closing out the series in the process.

When he eventually got out, the Windies only needed eight to win, and it also gave him the opportunity to soak in an ovation worthy of his man of the series award. He had been the difference, and though there were several on his side who had also put in excellent performances, his two centuries in three knocks was a tough act to match. We were still hurting, of course, but were looking forward to a week to re-energise. The second and third one-day matches had been played on consecutive days, so we barely had any time to let things soak in. Now, with a week before our first Test in two decades, we could get together as a team and really stress the importance of doing the basics right.

I must say that we all noticed the lift in intensity ahead of the Test match. There was no need for too much motivation, because this was the one thing that a lot of the players had been waiting for their entire careers. The World Cup was special, sure, but one-day international cricket was a format we were still getting to grips with. We had got as far as we did in Australia with heart, hunger and some luck and, when it ended, there was also an element of misfortune. There were no excuses in Test cricket, though. We had always privately felt that the Currie Cup competition wasn't too far off the intensity of the Test arena, because that is as hard as cricket got for most of our players. It was certainly full of personal duels and long-standing rivalries, and the excellent crowds that we enjoyed in domestic cricket back then gave the impression that this was as close to the real deal as we could get.

Naturally, we had also followed the international scene with interest. The West Indies were the dominant force of the 80s, with pace and swing, and plenty of quality batsmen. They had a swagger in their cricket, and for good reason, too. Any one of their top six could win a match with the bat, and their bowlers were also capable of a decisive swing of circumstances in one session. It was only one Test match, but it was a huge ask, especially at the back end of what we had already been through that season.

Naturally, every single one of our players wanted to be on the park, even more so than usual. This was historic, in a very different way to how India had been. This was a chance to make a statement, a sustained one at that, in the backyard of the most fearsome team in the world. The Windies had two debutants in their line-up, as Kenny Benjamin added to their pace attack, and keeper/batsman David Williams took his place behind the stumps. In contrast, we had ten players on debut, the odd one out being Kepler, from his years with Australia. We were a bundle of nerves and excitement, and we were very keen to bowl first, rather than bat. That may sound a bit negative to some, but our confidence wasn't at its peak after the one-dayers. We felt any bowler could come back and bowl another spell if his first one went wrong, but a bad session with the bat could see you lose the match, basically. The nature of the wicket also meant that the most life in the pitch was to be found on day one, when there was still some moisture. It was a sensible decision, and we were quite relieved when Kepler called correctly at the toss.

Before the game, both teams came together for a photo, and it was one that went around the world, for all the right reasons. We were all mixed in amongst each other, mutual respect across both sides, and there was a sense – at least in the picture – that the West Indies, the mighty powerhouse of modern cricket, was welcoming in the puppy to the litter. The tour itself had started off uneasily, with reservations on both sides about the timing. But, as we got together for that picture on the first morning, there was nowhere else we would rather be. The Kensington Oval was in pensive mood, and had been the scene of many a memorable contest. But the air was also heavy with drama because a large section had decided to boycott the match after Cummins hadn't been picked for the Test. He had been a handful during the one-day games, and he was unlucky not to be part of the Test match. It was hard to see where he could play, though. Ambrose and Walsh were certainties, and Kenny Benjamin had also troubled us in the one-dayers.

So, in a funny way, the crowd was initially a little friendlier towards us than the home side. It wasn't going to last forever, but we felt we had the chance to add to the folklore of the Kensington Oval with a one-off performance, before going home to reflect on what had been an incredible six months. The Test match itself was one of those remarkable matches, with an ending that perhaps summed up where we stood in terms of experience. We were right in it, to the point where a few of those travelling with the team felt certain that we would be signing off with a quite incredible upset victory. Of course, they had forgotten about two quicks named Curtly and Courtney, and the wicked way a Test match can switch in a session.

Things had started off well for the Windies, with Haynes and Simmons adding nearly 100 runs, and going quite breezily, too. Richard Snell then had the honour of claiming our first Test wicket in over 20 years, as he had Simmons caught by Peter Kirsten. Haynes followed him back, also to Snelly, and we had a sniff. But Keith Arthurton and skipper Richardson put on another decent stand, taking them over 200. With just three wickets down, it looked like they might just kick on to another massive total.

But, back came Snelly, and we were in business. He had Richardson caught behind, and Meyrick Pringle got rid of the dangerous Arthurton. We knew that there was very little beyond the keeper, Williams, who also happened to be on debut. Jimmy Adams spent an hour at the crease to make 11, until Donald castled him. For the first time on the tour, we felt on top in a match. What's more, we took advantage of the situation, too. We ran through their four-bowler tail, and suddenly a total that could have been 400 only realised 262 all out. Our decision to bowl first had been vindicated, and we just had to bat properly in our first dig. We knew that they would come hard at us in the few overs we had left before stumps, but Mark Rushmere and Hudders were very composed.

Hudders was someone who had worked hard on his game back home, and he had given a lot of credit to Henry Fotheringham, a veteran at Natal. 'Fothers' was part of a strong sporting culture, and his outlook on most situations was perfect for that of an opener. The time Hudders spent in the middle with him for Natal had clearly been beneficial, because Andrew started to play with authority and poise in the middle, even as he was confronted by two of the best fast bowlers of all time. His knock on the second day was the kind that openers dream of. Andrew was never one to be too outspoken. He kept to himself, but more than made up for his quiet demeanour with his determination on the field. Before the day had started, he had looked relaxed enough in the changing room, but we had no idea just how relaxed he was. His 163 was a great knock in any circumstances by a debutant. But, as an opener, in the cauldron of Barbados, against a four-pronged pace attack, it was immense. On form, he was very difficult to bowl to, because he could pull very well if you dropped short, but he was also a very good driver, especially down the ground.

The only pity was that Hudders received very little support from anyone else, bar Kepler. They put on 100 for the second wicket, but we didn't capitalise on the excellent platform as a team. Had we managed to add another 50 or so runs in our first innings, we may well have been out of sight. The pitch had already started to show signs of going up and down, and we knew that a meaningful target would be a very tough proposition in the fourth innings. Again, it may have been a lack of experience, but we gave four wickets to the part-time spin of Jimmy Adams, having done the hard yards against the quicks. That was especially frustrating, because Adams was Richie Richardson's last resort. Had we got past his left-arm spin, the Windies skipper would have had to go back to his big men before he wanted, and that could have even made a difference in the second innings.

The other thought that crept into the back of my mind was that we may have missed a trick not playing a spinner. The Caribbean is known as a haven for fast bowlers, but the pitch was breaking up, which would make a frontline spinner just as dangerous, especially in the second half of the match. It was another touch of inexperience in our side, because we perhaps didn't fully appreciate the position we almost put ourselves in.

That said, we had a handy lead of 83 when we were bowled out, and we still felt that the wicket was doing enough for us to perhaps roll them over. Snell and Donald were both still bowling beautifully. Allan seemed to be getting stronger, even after a long and emotionally draining season. They took a pair of wickets each, and we again had the game by the scruff of the neck. The home side were barely over 150, and six wickets down. Jimmy Adams, who had struggled for a run in the first innings, was all that stood between us and a target of little more than 100. By the close of play on day three, the Windies were still precariously placed at 184 for 7, a lead of 101. We then had a rest day, which probably worked against us.

We don't have rest days in modern Test cricket, but it was a regular occurrence back then. That extra day to ponder and plan was of little help, because all we really wanted to do was get back out there, and have a full go at Adams. But we had to stew for 24 hours, trying to take our minds off the very thing that we knew everyone else was thinking about. The guys were left to their own devices, generally, and we tried to keep things as relaxed as possible. No one needed reminding of the task that still lay ahead of us.

When we resumed play the next day, Adams looked like a man who hadn't stopped batting at all. We figured that it may take him a few overs to get back into his routine, and we were not sure how he was going to approach the session. He only had the tail with him, and they weren't known for even slogging. They could hang around at best, and eventually a ball would have their name on it. Adams was our priority, though. Would he slog? Would he farm the strike? Or would he just trust the bowlers to keep their end up, and bat as normal? These had all been discussed at length the day before, and we still had no idea. It would all unravel in the middle.

We didn't have to wait too long for the breakthrough. Allan had slowly pushed Benjamin on to the back foot, and finally trapped him leg-before. Our spearhead had done an outstanding job of putting his hand up as a future great, even in the company of giants like Ambrose and Walsh. They may not have known him a year earlier, but his exploits at the 1992 World Cup and on that trip certainly made them sit up and take notice. He was every bit as fast, and every bit as cranky as their fast bowlers, and he just lived for the big occasion. At 196 for 8, my mind started to look to the chase. A target of around 120 was always awkward, because it only took a few quick wickets for the nerves to set in. And, on a wicket that was deteriorating quickly, 120 was more like 180.

And yet, Adams and Walsh were still hanging on. Just before lunch, we finally got Walsh, caught behind for a very responsible 13. He had a peculiar style of leaving the ball, which the crowd absolutely loved, but it was infuriating for the bowler. You always felt he was about to nick it, but he just missed. When he finally feathered one through to Dave Richardson, we went to lunch with the feeling that we had already given them a few too many runs, but at least it was nearly over. And then Adams and Patrick Patterson decided to bat for over an hour and a half for the last wicket, putting on 62. It wasn't only the runs that hurt us; it was the frustration of not being able to put the innings to bed and get on with the chase. We tried plenty, and we again rued leaving out a spinner. But we couldn't cry over spilt milk. When we finally ended the stand-off, the Windies had added 109 for the last three wickets, and Adams's knock of 79 not out must have felt like a huge hundred for him and his team.

He had simply decided that he wasn't getting out, and barely played a false stroke. There was something to admire in that, and I remember feeling the same way when Steve Waugh decided to cut out the hook shot from his scoring options. He simply left, or ducked, or wore it, but he refused to allow himself to be dismissed in that fashion. That takes years of experience, and even disappointment, to realise that you need to make a change. In more recent years, we have seen South African batsmen save many a Test match by simply refusing to play a false stroke. There is an art to that, too, and that is what makes Test cricket so special. That knock by Jimmy Adams wasn't fluent, and wouldn't be up in lights, but it won the West Indies the match, because it gave them enough runs to get their bowlers fired up.

History will tell you that we lost that match by 52 runs, and legend will tell you that we lost it because we thought we had it won after day four, when we were 122 for 2, needing just another 79 runs for a famous win. I believe the truth lies somewhere in the middle of that. We had a very good platform, even after Hudders had got a second-baller from Ambrose. That's just cricket for you; a century in the first innings, and then a second-baller in the next. Mark Rushmere didn't last too long, but the partnership that Kirsy and Kepler then put up was excellent. They saw us through to the end of play, both patient and determined to see it through.

There are legends now that some of our guys were heard saying that they wouldn't even be needed, and that we had already started to plan the celebration. That was certainly not the case, or at least not as a collective. We had far too much respect for the Windies to assume that they would just roll over. We never ever assumed that we would just cruise to victory, and especially at the Kensington Oval. Even so, no one ever expected us to fold like a pack of cards. Ambrose was almost unplayable that day. He just hit the same spot, around off stump, and mixed it up with a few short balls every now and then to keep us honest. Once Kepler went as early as he did, they must have smelt a chance.

We still hoped that Kirsten would settle the ship, but he needed someone to stay with him. Hansie, Kuiper and Dave Richardson all nicked off. To think of all the times we had beaten the bat the day before, and yet we nicked everything we played at. The changing room was in a state of shock. It was a procession, and there was little time to prompt the next man in, because Ambrose simply scythed through us. We lost our last eight wickets for just 25 runs, and it was all over before we could try to make sense of it. Ambrose bowled Donald to complete the victory, and our first taste of Test cricket ended in complete shock.

The Windies went wild, of course. The boycott at the start of the match was forgotten, and Ambrose stood tallest, mobbed by his team-mates. We shook hands, and wandered back to the dressing room. It was a similar feeling to the semi-final against England just weeks before. We were learning some harsh lessons on our return to world cricket, and the latest one was especially hard to take.

But, we were back in the big time, and now we had an idea of just how much work lay ahead of us if we were to become a force in world cricket. The long road to the top had started.

Chapter 5

Athers, commentary, and the pain of '99

BEING COACH of South Africa as we made our way back on to the Test scene in the early 90s was very exciting. There was a bunch of players who were finding their feet, but we also had the experience of Kepler Wessels to lead us into this new age.

Having toured India to mark our return to the international fold, it was fitting that India were our first guests in a Test match, in late 1992. The match, at Kingsmead, was significant for several reasons, not least the fact that it was the first Test match on home soil since March 1970!

Another great significance in that match was Omar Henry becoming the first player of colour to play for South Africa, at the age of 40. Omar was a wily left-arm spinner, and had gone to the World Cup that year, too.

The third piece of history in that match – try and keep up – was Sachin Tendulkar being run out by Jonty Rhodes. The run-out was the first to be referred to the third umpire, as

Cyril Mitchley made the TV sign, and sent the decision to Karl Liebenberg to look over. That single moment changed the face of the game forever, as cricket made its first, tentative steps towards embracing technology.

With so much history around the occasion, you had to feel a bit sorry for poor old Jimmy Cook, who opened the batting for us. He bagged a first-baller on debut, as he nicked the very first ball of the match, from Kapil Dev, and was taken in the grabbers by Tendulkar!

Another interesting point from that match was the hamstring injury suffered by one of our bowlers, Brett Schultz. One of my great laments is that the world never got to see what I thought would have been one of the greatest ever bowling partnerships really flourish. Australia had Dennis Lillee and Jeff Thomson, the West Indies had Curtly Ambrose and Courtney Walsh – as well as countless other pairs in the 80s – England had Fred Trueman and Brian Statham, and I reckon that the history books would have been awash with Allan Donald and Brett Schultz, if the latter had managed to stay clear of injury.

I am sure there are still some players and spectators in Sri Lanka who get into a cold sweat at the mention of 'Schultzy', because he was absolutely devastating in 1993 there. Fast left-arm bowling is always tricky to deal with, and Brett Schultz was properly quick, and very aggressive!

He scythed through the islanders on our trip, and single-handedly won us the second Test in Colombo, after Jonty Rhodes had scored a ton to save us in the opening Test in Moratuwa. Schultz had already taken four wickets in the opening Test, and he then followed that up with 5-48 and 4-58, as we won by an innings and 208 runs.

Even on slow and low wickets, Schultz was a menace. He only knew one way to play – and that was all-out attack. To think that in later years, people thought that Donald and Dale Steyn were the South Africans with the wild eyes. If you could see Schultz running in, with war-paint and a growl on his face, you may have wanted to reconsider your lot in life.

He was player of the series in Sri Lanka against a team that had the likes of Arjuna Ranatunga, Aravinda de Silva, Sanath Jayasuriya and a young Muttiah Muralitharan in the ranks. He was in the face of the batsmen all the time, and didn't care much for saving runs. He just wanted the batsmen out, as soon as possible, and he left it all out on the pitch. Though we were a young side making our way in the Test ranks, I think the world would have taken notice far quicker if Schultz and Donald had five good years in cahoots.

But, sadly, his career was blighted by injury, and the world missed out on a bowling duo that would have been an uncompromising answer to Wasim and Waqar in the 90s. It was a real shame, but cricket goes that way sometimes. To see how far Allan Donald went in the game only serves to emphasise how formidable he and Schultz may have been together.

After Sri Lanka, out next big assignment was touring Australia, this time for the Test series. Sadly, our experience of the famous Boxing Day Test atmosphere was just about washed away, with big rain on the first two days, and the match eventually fizzled out into a damp draw. It was a real pity for the players, as a Test match in front of over 70 000 people – on day one alone – was not something that any of us, aside from Kepler, had ever experienced.

But even in the midst of all that rain, a fire had been sparked in Melbourne, as Daryll Cullinan and Shane Warne's career-long spat started. Legend has it that Daryll, standing at slip, had been quite lippy when Warne came in to bat, and the Aussie was definitely not going to forget it. As the years went by the war of words got more and more heated, and Warne certainly had the upper hand. He was a master of mind games, and he got into

Daryll's head. In later years, when South Africa played Australia again, Daryll did get one back, though. When Shane greeted him by telling him he had been waiting for years to bowl to him again, Daryll shot back a proper jab.

'Looks like you spent all that time eating!'

Even the Aussies around the bat had to laugh at that one. The second Test, of course, was to be known as the Fanie de Villiers Test, when he bowled us to victory on the final day. That tour was also the first encounter with Darrell Hair, but there is more on that, as well as Fanie's heroics and a bitter third Test in Adelaide, later on in these pages.

The series with Australia was ultimately shared, and they almost immediately came to South Africa for a return series. That series was also shared, as we won the opening Test at The Wanderers, with Hansie Cronje making a very good century, and several other contributions in the second innings helping us to an enormous 450, to set Australia a very unlikely 456 to win. We eventually won by 197 runs, though the match was marred by an incident involving Merv Hughes and a spectator, who gave him some advice as he went back to the dressing room. Merv responded by sticking his bat through the security gate, and The Wanderers have since made some adjustments to the players' tunnel on to the field!

The wonderful thing about those rivalries is that they tended to stay on the field – or at least the Aussies thought. During that Wanderers Test, our all-rounder Brian McMillan decided to play a practical joke on the Aussies. Security around both teams was pretty tight, so the last thing the Aussies expected was to see an AK47 being pointed at them.

Brian got one off the cops as a joke, and charged into the dressing room.

'Right, I am sick and tired of you Aussies! Where is that captain of yours, Border?!' he bellowed.

Mac had enjoyed a good tussle with Border, and eventually got him out. Border was a typical bulldog, and getting him was always a big blow. Mac was just lightening the mood, but apparently a few of our visitors went as white as a sheet! But it was all in jest, and we had a good chuckle in the next dressing room.

We lost the second Test in Cape Town despite making 360 in the first innings. Australia's warhorses, David Boon and Steve Waugh, both made telling contributions, and their response climbed beyond 450. Our second innings was a disaster, as we were rolled by Steve Waugh and his medium pace. We knew that the initials 'SW' would be a threat with the ball at Newlands, but we had figured on that being Shane Warne – and not Steve Waugh!

Australia only needed 90 to win, and they chalked it off with just one wicket down. So we went to Kingsmead all square, and still tied for the summer. It was all to play for, and we were feeling really positive when our middle order lifted us from 155 for 4 to 422 all out in our first dig. We had a lead of 153, but we had taken our time getting there.

Australia knew that there was only ever going to be one winner, and they saw out the rest of the Test match four wickets down, as a long summer of rivalry ended with handshakes – and a firm understanding that the teams were evenly matched.

It had been the first time I had crossed swords with Australia in a Test series since 1970 and, happily, the cricket remained just as fierce, even if we didn't have it our own way as we did back then!

As a massive summer signed off with some colourful one-dayers – which were hugely popular – my thoughts turned to the upcoming tour of England that winter. The build-up in England had already started, with just about every paper going on about the history that would be rewritten, and the resumption of a traditional rivalry.

More than that, we were going as the new South Africa. Nelson Mandela had been inaugurated in April 1994, and we were playing under our rainbow flag. It was a seismic shift in the country, and the entire tour was made even more special, given the historical links between the countries.

It was a big deal, and we were given massive press when we arrived there, too. For a long time, we had wondered if we would ever get the chance to play Test cricket again. To my mind – and I think several players agreed – a Test match at Lord's was the equivalent of playing something like The Masters, or going to the Olympics.

It was the pinnacle of the sport, and playing there almost always galvanised visiting teams to play above themselves. We had enjoyed a few warm-up games in the lead-up to the first Test, but nothing can prepare you for that first morning, especially for a batsman.

More than one player has got lost trying to make their way to the middle, and it can be a very daunting walk! The members are also very strict about the dress code at Lord's, and even the venerable Archbishop Desmond Tutu – a massive cricket fan – fell foul of the policy of jacket and tie on the occasion of our first visit there in decades.

Kepler had one of those days that every captain at Lord's wishes for. He won the toss and elected to bat first. He then proceeded to construct a solid century to see us to a handy total of 357. We had decided to go into the match with four seamers and no spinner. Allan Donald, who had played at Lord's on several occasions for Warwickshire, steamed in, and joined Kepler on the honours board, with 5-74.

We were all over them and we didn't relent in the second dig. Most of the batsmen chipped in for a total of 278 for 8 declared, leaving England with an impossible target of 456. We then skittled them for 99, to win by a most convincing 356 runs. I remember leaving four tickets for a mate of mine but he and his buddies had nipped out to see the town for a bit. They figured that they would come back at tea, and then return on day five for the end of the match. By the time they made it back to the ground, even the press conference had been done!

As convincing as our performance had been, most of the headlines in the aftermath centred on the naivety of Michael Atherton, the England skipper, which was a shame from our perspective. We had produced a thoroughly convincing performance, on a landmark occasion, and it felt a bit rough to be usurped by some dirt in the pocket.

Atherton had been caught, on camera, rubbing dirt on to the ball on day three, during our second innings. I had no idea at the time that it had happened, because I had been asked to go to the top of the Lord's pavilion to do an interview with Basil D'Oliveira. The rules around the dressing room were a lot more relaxed in those days, and I was just coming back from that interview when commentators Andre Bruyns and Trevor Quirk – who were there for the South African Broadcasting Corporation – asked me what we were going to do about it.

'Do about what?' I asked quizzically.

They then informed me about Athers being caught on camera with dirt in his pocket, and how it was all over the telly. They told me that they would get it for me, and I did my interview with Dolly. Once I was done, they showed it to me, and I didn't really know what to say. It was hard to see what Atherton was trying to do, and his subsequent explanation of trying to keep his hands and the ball dry were just as peculiar.

I went off to the opposition dressing room to see what their manager Ray Illingworth thought of it all. I had played with Ray for years, enjoying many battles against the very proud Yorkshireman. When I walked into the dressing room, it was empty. Ray and the rest of the coaching staff were on the balcony, watching the team in the field. Even the 12th man was out there with them, watching.

I called Ray aside, and told him that he should brace himself, because it looked like it would be quite serious. I am not sure if Ray thought much of it at the time, but he did eventually have a look on the screen. I was just trying to keep the peace and make sure that nothing overshadowed what was a massive week for us.

Of course, it did eventually blow up, and Illingworth saw fit to fine his skipper £2,000 for the whole affair once he had seen the replays himself. At the end of a grim match for England, Atherton was handed to the press, who went to town on it.

In our dressing room, I think there was a bit of disgruntlement that I hadn't made a bigger show of it. But, given the way we had played, I didn't see the point of worrying what the England captain was doing. In fact, I think it was Graham Gooch who summed it up best, when he commented on the condition of the ball being altered.

'Well, it must have been theirs, because ours did **** all!'

We knew that England would look to bounce back, and Atherton himself came back at us with a stoical 99 in the second Test at Headingley. In fact, were it not for some fine batting by Peter Kirsten and nightwatchman Dave Richardson, we may well have lost. The pitch was not great, and Kirsy's 104 was a thing of true grit. He kept our noses in front, and Dave's 48 was worth a whole lot more to us in the circumstances.

We got to The Oval one good result away from sealing the series, but there were issues in the background. Before the tour, convenor of selectors Peter Pollock and I had decided that Kepler would hand over the captaincy to Hansie Cronje at the end of the England tour. It was a natural succession, and Kepler was happy with the arrangement. Hansie had proved himself, not least in Sydney, when he deputised for an injured Kepler and led us to that famous five-run win.

But, over the course of the England tour, Hansie had become withdrawn, as he struggled for runs in a big series. I saw that as a sign that maybe he wasn't quite ready to take over a huge responsibility from Kepler, and suggested to Peter that maybe we hold him back for a bit.

Hansie must have got wind of my thinking, and perhaps took it the wrong way. I was actually trying to protect him for a bit longer, but he may have assumed that I was suggesting he was the wrong man for the job.

There was a one-day tour to Pakistan not long after the England trip, and it involved a triangular with Australia. I thought Hansie may be better served getting back into form and then taking over the reins in the summer. The last thing I wanted was for him to walk into a job and be up against it from the first ball.

As it was, Peter agreed with me, and Kepler was happy to hold on for a bit longer. But, before all that, we needed to play five days of good cricket at The Oval. It turned out to be one of the crazier matches that I have been involved in.

Everything was a blur. We made runs in a hurry, and lost wickets at an even brisker rate. Our first innings was characterised by Jonty being hit on the head by Devon Malcolm, the big fast bowler who could really let it go. Jonty, ducking into one that was a bit lower than he may have hoped, was clattered really hard, and was taken to hospital.

I went with him, and he was in a really bad way. In hindsight, we should never have let him take the field again – especially not to bat in the second innings. I shudder at the thought of what may have happened if he had been struck again, especially after Malcolm's cage was rattled by Fanie de Villiers.

Though we had let Darren Gough and Phil DeFreitas get away with some easy runs, we still felt in control of the match at that point, with a lead of about 30. When Malcolm got hit on the helmet by Fanie, things took a wicked turn for the worse. Legend has it that he had a message for the fielders who gathered around him.

'You guys are history,' he apparently said.

What followed was one of the fastest, most hostile spells of fast bowling any of us had ever seen. Malcolm was angry, and he took it out on us that day. We were one run for three wickets at one stage as he blew right through our top order. We were deer in the headlights, but there was one man who gave us hope.

Daryll Cullinan is much maligned for his history with Shane Warne, but on that day at The Oval he played a knock that never got the credit it fully deserved. Against proper fast bowling, he was all class, and his 94 deserved to be three figures. We were eventually bowled out for 175, setting England 204 to square the series.

We were still recovering from the shock, and Graham Gooch saw a chance to go hard up front. Allan Donald went for 96 in just 12 overs, and the chase was over in the blink of an eye. England only needed 36 overs, which says everything about our state of mind. We bowled terribly, and our hopes of winning our first series back on English soil disappeared on one crazy afternoon.

After that match we had an engagement in Holland, with a one-off one-dayer against the Dutch. Even before the English tour, it had been decided that some of the touring party – including myself – didn't have to go to Amsterdam. So, we stayed behind as the team went off to honour their fixture.

Of course, with one foot on the plane home, we were embarrassed by Holland, and what had been a great tour ended on a very poor note. There was a sting in the tale for me soon after we arrived home.

There had been speculation that I may lose my job as coach of South Africa, but I hadn't heard anything from the top. I had heard that Allan Donald was quite keen on Bob Woolmer, who he had worked with closely at Warwickshire, and I sensed that things between Hansie and I had become a bit frosty.

But, I had my own problems at the time. I had been rushed to hospital with a terrible pain near my heart. The nurses all thought it was a heart attack, but thankfully the specialist, Dr Dave Gilmer, correctly diagnosed it as inflammation of the muscles around the heart – a small but critical difference.

I was in the intensive care unit at St Augustine's when the decision was made to sack me as national coach. Ali, as a friend, thought to let me know before it made the morning news. Some questioned his timing but I appreciated the gesture, and I took his call.

It had been a heck of an experience coaching the side back into the international fold, and I had some incredible moments, good and bad. It is never fun being fired, I suppose, but it is one of the absolute certainties of coaching or managing in sport.

Funnily enough, the team went to the triangular in Pakistan, and proceeded to lose all six matches. Hansie, playing without the burden of captaincy just yet, enjoyed a good series with the bat. So perhaps there was a bit of method to my cautionary madness, after all.

As it so happened, the coaching door closing on me meant that other doors would soon be open down the line. Barely a year later, a friend of mine suggested that I should try my hand – or voice – at commentating. I didn't have a clue how one went about getting a gig behind the mic, but I soon had a phone call that made it all rather simple.

'Do you want a job?' the voice on the other end enquired.

I obviously said yes, and the instruction followed.

'Expect a call from John Gayleard.'

The voice on the other end was Sam Chisholm, a media executive of real significance in sports broadcasting. In no time,

I was in the Sky Sports box for the return series of England in South Africa, alongside Michael Holding, David Gower and Ian Botham.

I was petrified because there was little or no training, and these guys around me made it look so natural. I must have said something right, because I stuck around until I became an ICC match referee at the turn of the century.

I went on most of the trips, following England home and abroad. They were good times, with guys who knew the game and were well respected. I had played with or against most of them, which made conversation very natural.

It also opened my eyes up to a completely different avenue in the game. Having played and coached, I now could appreciate what a commentator could bring to the overall product. Satellite television was booming, and Sky was at the forefront of that. We had some cracking times in the studio, and I always felt the balance between analysis and banter was just right. It never felt like work, in a sense.

A particular highlight for me was the 1999 World Cup, which was obviously a massive operation for Sky to produce. As the tournament reached its climax, we were all pretty nervous. The semi-final between South Africa and Australia has gone down as one of the greatest sporting contests ever, and it was a privilege to be there.

I just wish we had managed one more run. I had coached most of the players in that team, and I would have loved for them to get over the line. I thought South Africa bowled brilliantly to confine Australia to just 213. It was definitely under par on a good Edgbaston wicket.

But Shane Warne was incredible, and his spell of 4-29 was the game changer. We could sense it was going to be a ding-dong battle to the end, but no one could have foreseen the end. Lance Klusener had shown himself to be a Superman during that tournament, and it looked like he was about to single-handedly win the World Cup.

The producers had already given us the roster, and it had Bill Lawry and I calling the final half an hour of play. It was riveting, and South Africa looked like they had it sewn up when Klusener crashed the first two balls of Damien Fleming's over for four, leaving them just one run to get – with four balls still remaining.

And then, the unthinkable, as there was a near run-out the ball before, and then the calamity the next ball. Bill and I had been quite animated on air, but I actually went numb when that run-out occurred. I couldn't believe it, and Bill carried on, telling the world about the greatest one-day game ever seen.

I didn't think anyone deserved to lose. And, actually, South Africa didn't lose. But no one remembers it like that and, of course, Australia went on to claim the World Cup. I remember going into the South African dressing room and it honestly felt like walking into a funeral.

There was genuine pain in there, and I felt for them, too, just as every South African, I am sure. There were tears, there were blank faces, and there was an eerie silence. I felt pretty much the same.

I told the studio guys that I would make my own way back to the hotel, and I couldn't get a taxi in the madness that followed. So I walked back, which took me at least 45 minutes. Even then, when I got back into my room, I was still numb.

Cricket has given me some wonderful memories, but that 1999 World Cup semi-final will always rank as one of the darkest days for me as a South African.

I still can't believe it.

Chapter 6

Monkeygate and the mess that followed

WHEN I became an international match referee in 2002, I was looking forward to what I saw to be the final chapter of my career. I had been a player, a coach, a manager, and also did stints of commentary. The role of match referee was something that appealed to me, because you were still a part of the action, if not quite in the middle as an umpire.

Of course, my 47 Test matches as a match referee included some of the most controversial moments the game has seen. None of those had a bigger impact, or the consequences felt more deeply, than the Monkeygate scandal of 2008.

India against Australia has always been a fixture that world cricket looked forward to, and the 2007/08 tour Down Under by Anil Kumble's men was much anticipated. It was a clash of cultures and playing styles, and one that I was excited to be a small part of. After the turn of the century, these two nations had served up some of the greatest matches and series in recent memory.

I remember catching the tail end of the remarkable turnaround by VVS Laxman and Rahul Dravid in 2001, when they followed on and stunned the Aussies. It was breathless stuff, and I could just imagine how the capacity crowds must have celebrated that victory long into the night.

Much of India's success in that 2001 series was owed to a young off-spinner by the name of Harbhajan Singh, who took an astonishing 32 wickets in just three Test matches. His battle with Australia's left-handers was a joy to watch, and that series did a lot for advancing the game forward as a thrilling spectacle.

Australia had come into the series on the back of 15 successive Test victories, and they looked unstoppable. That India managed to come back from following on, already one down in the series, and still win was an incredible effort. Though some of the central figures in the incredible series of 2001 were not around anymore, it was still a compelling cast.

I had been match referee in 2003/04 when India had last visited Australia on a full tour for the Border-Gavaskar Trophy. Both sides have always been blessed with exceptional stroke-players, who always looked to take the game to the opposition. Added to attacking field settings, it meant that there was never a dull moment, and very few draws.

Back in late 2003, after a drawn first Test, one of the true gentlemen of the game took centre stage in Adelaide. Rahul Dravid, who remains one of the most respected voices in the game, took the second Test by the scruff of the neck with a brilliant 233, in response to Ricky Ponting's 242 in Australia's first dig.

Dravid didn't always have the fluency of a Tendulkar or a Ponting, but when he was set at the crease, few players looked more impossible to get out. Australia threw everything at him, but there was no budging him. His 72 in the second innings saw

India chase down the 230 they had been set, having rolled the Aussies over for 196, thanks to a fine spell of swing bowling from Ajit Agarkar.

I remember Dravid being first introduced to South Africa back in 1997. His international career was only a few months old, but he made his maiden Test century in the final Test at the Wanderers, and followed it up with 81 in the second innings. What immediately struck us about him was that he was very technically correct, and quite enjoyed the ball coming on to him. The nickname 'the Wall' was very apt, even in the early stages.

Later on in that 2003/04 series, India's biggest star made his presence felt. Sachin Tendulkar had been quiet all series long, as Australia kept on inducing edges from him. Frustrated by the lack of runs, the Indian fans had started to get on his case.

That was another remarkable aspect of India in Australia. They managed to be one of the very few teams who seemed to have as many fans as the home side in the stands. When they were on top, with bat or ball, they drowned out the locals, especially in Sydney and Melbourne.

By the time the fourth Test in Sydney came around, Australia were back in the contest, after winning the Boxing Day Test by eight wickets. Somehow, India had contrived to waste Virender Sehwag's blistering 183, to fall from 350 for 4 to 366 all out. Ponting, having the summer of his life, made 257 as the hosts piled up more than 500. I always enjoyed the way Ponting batted. He was always looking to take the game forward, and those back-to-back double hundreds confirmed him, in my mind at least, as one of the true greats.

There was no way back for India, and the scene was set for a final showdown in Sydney. The occasion was made all the more memorable because it was Steve Waugh's final Test. He had been a terrific servant for Australian cricket, as well as an ambassador for

Test cricket and its legacy. Nothing would have given the Aussies more joy than to send him into the sunset with one last hurrah.

Of course, no one had told India about that. Tendulkar, as great players tend to do, saved his best for the biggest occasion. His 241 was a masterclass in concentration, because he simply didn't hit anything through the off side. It was remarkable. The Aussies, who had got him caught behind several times, dangled the carrot, but he wouldn't bite.

Instead, he waited for them to go a touch straighter, and then belted it down the ground, or used his wrists to go through the leg side. It was batting of the highest order, impregnable and a timely reminder that he remained one of the best to ever play. Sure, Australia were missing Shane Warne and Glenn McGrath, but an attack of Jason Gillespie, Brett Lee, Nathan Bracken and Stuart MacGill was not one that most Test-playing countries would scoff at.

Tendulkar's stand of 353 with Laxman saw India rack up over 700, but I thought they batted a touch too long, and thus cost themselves the chance to win the series outright. Waugh said goodbye in defiant style, with an 80 that made sure his side wouldn't lose his final Test. Australia ended six down, and a series high on quality and runs was shared by two quality teams, who had played in the right spirit.

So when I was assigned to be match referee in the 2007/08 series, I still had fond memories of packed stadiums, a host of quality players, and the promise of another thrilling series. Of course, I had absolutely no idea that things were about to take a controversial turn, with me caught squarely in the middle.

The first Test of the 2007/08 series was on Boxing Day, and again Australia found themselves on the verge of history. Their great side of the early 2000s had set a high bar, but as the likes of Shane Warne, Glenn McGrath, Justin Langer and Damien Martyn had followed Steve Waugh into retirement, the Aussies had somehow built another great side, led by Ponting. The opening Test against India gave them the chance to make it 15 Test wins in a row.

Matthew Hayden had given the home side the perfect start, with another typical century up front. The manner in which Australia have advanced scoring rates in Test cricket especially is down to players like Hayden, who are always looking to put bowlers on the back foot. He was physically intimidating, and I had noted before that he hit the ball every bit as hard, and as straight, as Graeme Pollock used to do when we played.

Hayden and Phil Jaques had given Australia a perfect start, a century stand at four runs an over, but the rest of the team didn't cash in, as they were bowled out for 343, thanks to captain Anil Kumble's five-wicket haul, and Zaheer Khan's swing bowling.

As a match referee, your job is determined by what happens in the middle. Most games rattle along with no real drama, so you can get absorbed into the contest. Watching India fight back like that showed that they were here to try and stop the Aussie domination, but also perhaps to win the series that they had almost claimed in 2004.

Things took a dramatic turn on day two, as the visitors were bowled out for just 196. India had rejigged their batting line-up to include Yuvraj Singh in the middle order. It meant Rahul Dravid had to go up and open the batting. He went into his shell, scoring at a very slow rate, and things were not helped by Yuvraj then getting out for a duck. The left-hander hung around when he was adjudged caught behind off Stuart Clark by Billy Bowden. It was in the midst of the Indian crumble and, having been drafted into the side primarily for his batting, Singh looked gutted with himself. He stood around for a while, looking shocked at the decision. Billy and Mark Benson took that as a show of dissent, and charged him with breaching Level 1.3 of the Code of Conduct, which is showing dissent by action or verbal abuse.

The hearing was held at the end of the third day, by which time Australia had already declared their second innings, and set India 499 to win. Skipper Anil Kumble, Yuvraj Singh, India's team manager Chetan Chauhan and the four umpires were present at the hearing, and we pulled up video evidence from day two.

I reiterated my initial stance to all concerned. I thought Yuvraj had hung around for a bit longer than usual, but I also felt that he had not shown any actual dissent to the umpires. There was a fine line between disappointment and dissent, but I thought Yuvraj's actions had fallen into the former category. He was shocked at the decision, but there was a noise, and the appeal was spontaneous from behind.

He was cleared of the charge, and he apologised for his actions to the umpires. There were handshakes all around, and the focus went back to the cricket, which Australia duly wrapped up the next day. Naturally, I was relieved with the way that the Yuvraj incident had played out. As a referee, you never ever want to be mentioned, because your anonymity is usually a sign that things are going along smoothly.

Australia celebrated that victory heartily. It meant that they were one win away from equalling their world record of 16 wins on the trot – the same one that India had snapped in 2001 – and they had also given everyone involved an extra day off to relax.

Melbourne is one of the great cities in the world, especially at that time of the year. The match ended not long after tea, which meant that by the time all the post-match ceremony was done, we were still in good time to go out for supper and a quiet drink, in reflection of a good Test match.

My wife was only arriving during the Sydney Test, so I had a drink after supper, and went off to bed happy with the first Test. The Yuvraj incident wasn't even a footnote in the papers the next day, and that was a relief.

Sydney was on the horizon now, and that was always a nice place to visit. To get there in time for New Year's Eve was also a treat, because the whole place just comes alive. The lot of a life in cricket can be tough, but it is hard to complain when you happen to be in a place like Sydney for New Year, and there is another big Test match on the horizon.

Quite how big I would only find out over the course of the next week. It was to prove to be the beginning of the end of my career as a match referee, and that ugliest of human diseases, racism, was the catalyst for all the madness that became that first week of 2008.

Much has been said and written about the incident involving Harbhajan Singh and Andrew Symonds, because it was a personal duel that had a lot of history. Symonds had previously accused the Indian spinner of racial abuse in Mumbai, and they unsurprisingly didn't have much time for each other.

Of course, both players were crucial to their teams, especially in this particular match. Symonds' century in the first innings had saved Australia's blushes, and then transferred the pressure on to India. Tendulkar, as he so often did, answered the call for India, with a magnificent century.

Just when it looked like he was running out of partners, Harbhajan stuck around defiantly, mixing aggression with application. It was a terrific partnership, just the type that Australia didn't want, but one that the match needed.

I can still see Ricky Ponting bounding off the field, and up the stairs in a real hurry. This usually meant an injured finger or, more likely, nature's call can't wait for the approaching tea break. But it was infinitely more serious than that.

Symonds, who had been fielding at mid-off with Brett Lee bowling, had exchanged words with Harbhajan at the non-striker's end, and he was adamant that the spinner had called him a 'monkey'. It was a massive allegation, given all the efforts that the ICC had undertaken to eradicate racism from the game, and encourage participation from all corners of the globe.

Ponting ran straight into the home dressing room, and informed the team manager. He came across to me, and said they fully intended on laying a charge, and that Symonds was very upset. I had seen the players coming together, and assumed it was regular banter between two men playing the game hard.

Racism was the last thing that I had initially thought of, because the ICC had made such a concerted effort to ensure that everyone inside a cricket stadium knew the stance on racist abuse. It was not to be tolerated, from anyone, and there were posters all around each venue reminding fans and everyone at the game that they had a code to adhere to. One of my responsibilities was to make sure that the posters were clearly visible at strategic points around the ground.

When Tendulkar and a few of the close-in fielders – including Ponting – stepped in, however, I thought it might be a bit more than the usual chirping. Ponting's dash off the field confirmed the suspicion, and the die was cast soon after. The umpires came into their room at tea, and said that Ponting had told them what Symonds had said.

Neither one of the umpires had heard the conversation, and nor had Ponting. Tendulkar also hadn't heard anything, but Adam Gilchrist and Matthew Hayden were sure they had heard it. Things were escalating in a hurry, but play resumed after tea, and the match unfolded into quite a thriller, with Australia dramatically winning in the final over.

The hearing was set for the end of play on day five, and due to the seriousness of the situation, India were told that they could bring in a legal representative from Sydney or fly one in from India for assistance. The team managers had also had the opportunity beforehand to meet with Nigel Peters QC, whose assistance had been requested by the ICC.

It took a while for things to settle down immediately after the match. The Australian team was still changing, and there was still a lot of emotion from what had been a tense finish in the match. We felt a bit like two boarding masters trying to restore order before lights out.

One of the things that always stuck with me about the entire case was the lack of readiness regarding so many crucial elements. Firstly, we had a tape of the incident in question, but the sound had somehow disappeared. Given that the entire case rested on what had been said, it was not the greatest start.

In our quickly assembled hearing venue, there was also no recording device, or even anyone taking down an official record. The final straw for me was in the appeal hearing that followed a few days later, when the judge who overturned the decision admitted that he had not been given any documents regarding Harbhajan's previous misdemeanours – including Mumbai – and went as far as saying that his decision would have been different if he had the full picture.

I am glad to say that things have changed since then, and the laws pertaining to such incidents and hearings have since been changed. A hearing of such a serious nature can no longer be held by a match referee, but by an appointed legal counsel, be it a QC or a judge appointed by the ICC. But we were definitely on the back foot in that sense. The ICC followed English law, and so the hearing took the pattern of a trial.

The hearing itself lasted about three hours, but it felt even longer because Nigel Peters QC and I had spent the final hour of the Test match frantically trying to organise a venue for the hearing. There was nowhere to go really, and the way that the SCG is set up, we eventually decided to do it in the dining room.

Nigel, who was a member of the London Bar and also a member of the MCC committee, had been requested by the ICC to assist me in terms of procedure and any legal matters that could arise. It wasn't the ideal place, given the boisterous celebrations by the home side after a tense win in the final over of the game, but we just got on with it, and we never even thought of asking too many of the staff to help.

Australia's contingent consisted of Andrew Symonds, captain Ponting, keeper Adam Gilchrist, and witnesses Matthew Hayden and Michael Clarke, as well as their team manager, Steve Bernard. Present for India were Harbhajan, skipper Anil Kumble, witness Sachin Tendulkar, team manager Chetan Chauhan and the assistant manager Dr MV Sridhar.

The match on-field umpires, Steve Bucknor and Mark Benson, were also in attendance. The formal evidence started, with the umpires confirming Australia had to give their evidence first, confirming that an incident had been reported to them on day three, by Ricky Ponting. The Aussie skipper was the first witness, and he said that he had been told by his players that they had heard Harbhajan calling Symonds a monkey.

The Indian manager, Chetan, was then invited to ask Ponting any questions relating to the matter, which he duly did. His question was more of an allegation, as he accused Australia of making up the whole racism incident, simply because they wanted Harbhajan off the tour, because he kept getting Ponting out.

The entire Australian party was stunned by the allegation, but Chetan was not done just yet. He informed Ponting that the racism charge was completely made up, because as Indians, it was just not possible for them to be racist.

I was staggered because, in my world experience, I had seen racism from all corners, regardless of culture. Australia had come to me with an allegation against India, and the visiting team had done nothing to counter that serious allegation. My job was to rule on the matter given the evidence provided. On that count, India's silence left me with very little choice. To throw out Australia's charge on the assumptive grounds that it was impossible for India to be racist would have made a mockery of the entire hearing. I was simply doing my job to the best of my abilities, and India never once defended or explained what had happened out in the middle.

I didn't quite know where he was headed next, but Chetan then produced an album of photos, with princes and princesses in regal dress, but with monkey heads. He said that monkeys were an Indian deity, further reiterating their point that the entire episode had been made up, because they wouldn't want to insult monkeys.

Once the room had settled down from that opening salvo, Clarke and Hayden testified that they had both heard the word said. The cross-examination for both of them basically centred on the fact that they simply weren't telling the truth.

Gilchrist said he hadn't heard it, but went back to an incident in Mumbai, where Harbhajan had called Symonds a monkey, and apologised. The pair had shaken hands back then, and the matter was considered closed at that point.

Harbhajan was then invited to give his evidence, but Chetan, the team manager, responded by saying that his spinner wouldn't be testifying, because he didn't speak English. For the second time, several people in the room were left absolutely astounded.

Nigel Peters QC then said we were happy for Harbhajan to give evidence in his native tongue, and then get one of the present party to translate. Tendulkar, or Kumble or even Chetan himself all spoke very good English – as did Harbhajan, or so I thought until the hearing.

It was important for him to give some sort of testimony, obviously. India were adamant that he was not giving evidence. I was no law expert, but the simple logic was that there was only one side prepared to give their version of the story.

Nigel Peters QC also asked Sachin Tendulkar, who was the other batsman, if there was any chance that he had heard anything. Tellingly, Tendulkar said he couldn't hear anything from where he was, and that was quite understandable. The Sydney Cricket Ground holds over 40,000 people, and it must be almost impossible to hear each other out in the middle without shouting.

If the umpire hadn't heard it, there was every chance that Sachin hadn't either. He only walked towards his partner when he saw that something was up. Tendulkar's subsequent insistence – at the appeal – that he had very clearly heard Harbhajan say 'teri ma ki chut', an abusive, but not racist, term in Hindi, baffled everyone who was at the initial hearing.

Ricky Ponting said as much in his autobiography a few years later, sharing the astonishment that Tendulkar, one of the great voices of world cricket, didn't state this when first invited to do so during the hearing.

It goes without saying that his belated evidence would have changed my judgement on the incident, given the plausibility of it. The words 'monkey' and 'ma ki', heard 22 yards away, must sound very similar, and that entire episode could have been a high-profile case of lost in translation. But Tendulkar never came forward with that version to us in the initial hearing, which left me with very little choice.

Australia had several witnesses, all of whom were adamant that they had heard it. We replayed the video to check proximity, and given that they were very close to Harbhajan and Symonds, you couldn't rule out that they could hear the conversation. After all, it was highly unlikely that the pair would have been whispering to each other.

India, on the other hand, offered absolutely nothing in terms of evidence. Instead, they came with allegations of a witch-hunt, including that incredible assessment that Ponting wanted Harbhajan out of the series for his own benefit. They gave me absolutely no defence and, subsequently, little alternative when it came to deciding on the matter.

I went to the umpires' room to consider my verdict. At the back of my mind, I guess I had been hoping that there would be reasonable doubt that there had been any racial abuse involved. However, Australia had several witnesses who were adamant, and India gave nothing to refute the narrative.

It was a weighty matter, and one that had serious implications. A player had been accused of racial abuse, and several witnesses had confirmed that they had heard it. The defendant, in this case, had simply shouldered arms. I had a job to do, but I could only do it with the evidence that had been put in front of me.

What really confused me is why India were going so far out of their way to make matters difficult. To say that Harbhajan didn't speak English already bordered on the farcical, but to then offer no counter argument to the Aussies' accusations was beyond belief. I couldn't understand it. If someone accused me of anything – especially something as serious as racism – I would stand up and defend myself vehemently.

Harbhajan simply said nothing, and left me with very little to work with. I sat for about half an hour, more in confusion at India's stance in the hearing. I called in the judge to help me draft my findings, and then we called both parties in. It was already past midnight by then. The initial hearing had lasted about three hours, so by the time we sat down for the handing down of the verdict, it was close to 2am the next morning. By the time I got back to my hotel, the sun was starting to rise again. It had been, by all accounts, a very long night.

I informed of my guilty verdict, and then went through the reasons for my decisions. As we were utilising English law, one of the premises is that guilt is concluded if something is argued beyond reasonable doubt, which I felt had been the case in this matter. The verdict was met with silence, and so we moved on to the matter of sentence. I had the discretion of imposing a ban of up to three Test matches, which I went with. I felt the matter was that serious, and the lack of counter evidence from India reinforced the fact that he was guilty.

Though we couldn't get our hands on a copy of Harbhajan's previous misdemeanours, a single act of racial abuse was punishable by a three-match ban, because the governing body of the sport took the subject that seriously.

The fallout was unsurprisingly heated. The press were scathing in their appraisal of the situation. The late Peter Roebuck – a writer who was respected worldwide – asked why the ICC had let Australia get away with acting like a pack of dogs, and bemoaned us for targeting a man (Harbhajan) who was feeding a family of nine through the game.

I felt that the press had got the wrong end of the stick. In hindsight, I almost wish the facts had been put out in public, in order for them to form an enlightened opinion on proceedings. I was later quoted as saying 'only one team is telling the truth', or words to that effect.

Though I can't remember saying those exact words, I can certainly recall thinking that only one team was playing ball, if you will. India simply didn't budge from their initial allegations to Ponting, and didn't bother producing any evidence to defend Harbhajan, or at least counter the allegations levelled against him.

Former Indian batsman Sunil Gavaskar, who I had considered a friend from our duels in our playing days, tore into me in the papers, too. He said I was always going to go against the brown man, when he was up against the white man. I took that quite personally, because it was a massive generalisation, and one that went against every bit of my moral fibre.

In India, one newspaper depicted the match officials, including yours truly, and the central characters in the Australian team as the nine-headed evil god. It was taken as a slight against the entire nation, and I was suddenly persona non grata. There were even some former Indian players, who I had got along with

In full flight at Bristol, against Hampshire in 1977.

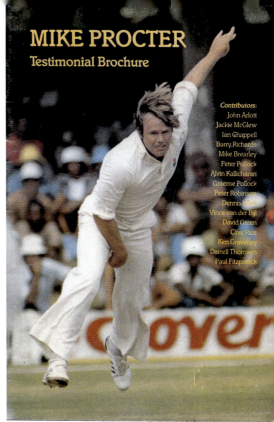

My benefit brochure.

My wife Maryna, in her prime as a tennis player on the world tour.

An article on the Newlands Walk-off in 1971, when we left the field after just one ball.

The Newlands Walkoff

A great Test side. Who knows what this South African unit could have achieved.

Toast of the town: Celebrating our 1977 Benson and Hedges Cup win with the Mayor of Gloucester and his family, along with team-mate Andy Stobold.

Stellar cast: Double-wicket competition in Bristol, featuring (from left) Zaheer Abbas and I, against Ian Botham and Viv Richards.

January 2017 with Garry Sobers and good friend Rod MacSween in Barbados. Rod is a hugely successful music agent who represents among others, Guns n Roses, Lenny Kravitz, The Who, Pearl Jam and Aerosmith.

Bowling against Worcestershire in the 1973 Gillette Cup semi-final at New Road.

A great day for Gloucestershire. Celebrating the 1973 Gillette Cup triumph over Sussex, with the team hoisting yours truly and skipper Tony Brown aloft.

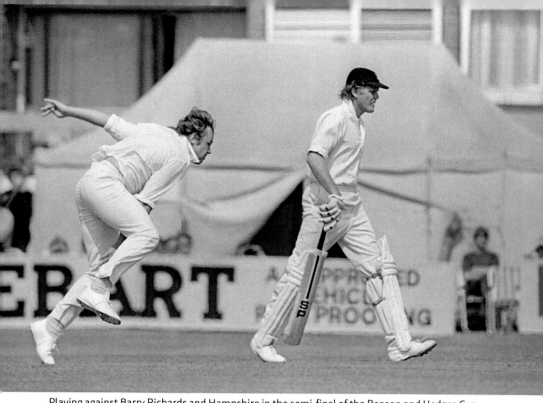

Playing against Barry Richards and Hampshire in the semi-final of the Benson and Hedges Cup, in 1977.

Close but no cigar. Calming down the crowd after losing the County Championship on the last day of the 1977 season.

My Rolls-Royce being given the once over by Natal team-mate and long-time friend, Tich Smith (far left). Tich has done wonderful work over the years with his LIV Foundation.

Happy days in Chiang Mai, playing a Sixes tournament. The hospitality in Thailand was phenomenal.

Cup glory with Northamptonshire, with a certain Curtly Ambrose as our star man.

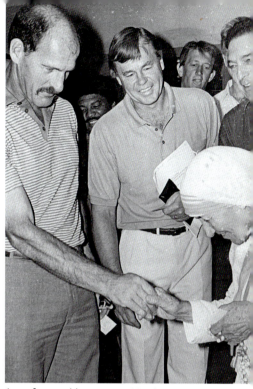

Shorts and suits. Ali Bacher was instrumental in getting South Africa back into international cricket. This was a quiet moment during our historic tour of India.

An unforgettable moment: Meeting Mother Teresa during our tour of India in 1991.

1994, a great return to cricket at Lord's, complete with some boisterous celebrating on the balcony.

Getting the boys sharp on the field during the 1994 tour to England.

Coaching the national team in 1994 was thirsty work.

Doing my bit for the media as team coach during the 1994 tour.

The scene outside the Sheraton Hotel, which was across the road from our hotel in Karachi. A bomb in a bus exploded outside the Sheraton, and killed 12 people.

The carnage outside the Sheraton, and the beginning of the end for international cricket in Pakistan.

The effects from the bomb blast in Karachi. My room was on the sixth floor.

Inspecting the scene in my hotel room in Karachi.

All-rounders united. Chatting to Jacques Kallis during my days as national selector.

Having a word with former England captain, Michael Vaughan.

The calm before the storm. Watching Andrew Strauss and Inzamam-ul-Haq toss up in the early stages of the walk-off Test in 2006.

Catching up with my old mate and Pakistan great Zaheer Abbas, a friendship that stretches back decades.

One of the more unsubtle images that were generated in India after the Monkeygate scandal.

Commentating was a part of my cricketing journey that I really enjoyed.

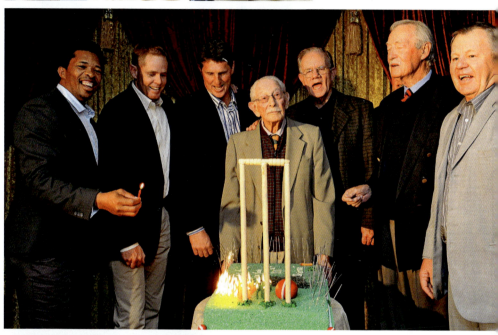

A few South African cricket legends gathered for the 100th birthday of Norman Gordon, at The Longroom, at the Wanderers, back in 2011.

Charity: In conversation with Sir Victor Blank, a good friend and a philanthropist of great significance to the game.

My other great pastime – playing golf, at the treacherous Wild Coast Sun layout.

Springbok giant lock, Mark Andrews, and I in the rough at the Wild Coast Sun. It was probably his ball that was lost, rather than mine!

A touching letter from the Soweto Cricket Club.

SOWETO
CRICKET·CLUB

Mr Mike Procter
Fax: 031 300-0076

24 November 1997

Dear Mike

Please pardon me for opening with a prayer, I want to get my facts right. "O Lord, you have done so many things for me, please give me one more thing, a grateful heart".

"We are proud of your team" people I meet in cricket circles, say. My conscience worries me, because they are showering us with praises, which rightly should be directed to you.

It is better late than never. I was a victim of circumstances. It was the old story. "Whose job was it, to thank him"? Yesterday I asked the people who had to do it. "So and so was supposed to do it".

We walk tall all because of you. If your memory serves you well, you will remember what I said after you and Jeff had addressed the Soweto cricketers. " Gentlemen, I thank you for arming our boys for the coming season. I'm positive that they will not encounter any problems because you have given them everything they will need".

We have not lost a single match in the Premier League. I feel, whatever I may say, in trying to thank you, will fall short of the praise you so richly deserve, so let my simple thank you suffice.

Yours sincerely

L. Mvumvu

Lawrence Mvumvu
Soweto Cricket Club

PO Box 134, Dube, Soweto, 1800

Chairman: R. Baladinvithu   Home Tel: (011) 988 8183   Work & Fax No: (011) 933-3229

The Mike Procter Foundation project at the Ottawa Primary School using cricket as a vehicle to improve self-esteem and as an escape from the realities of daily life.

With coach Rodney Malamba and the Ottawa Primary School children.

From left: Shane Warne, me, Rod MacSween, Allan Lamb and Robin Smith. Taken at Sir Victor Blank/Sir David Frost Annual cricket match for Wellbeing of Women.

famously before that fateful Sydney Test, who have given me considerably short shrift ever since that day.

I still wonder what version of the story these people heard or read. I was left to hand down a verdict based on the evidence I was given. I was simply doing my job with the tools that I had been handed. To this day, I still cannot understand why Tendulkar said he didn't hear anything at the end of the Test match, and was suddenly so sure of what he had heard a few days later, at the hearing.

India refused to leave Sydney, and immediately signalled their intentions to appeal my verdict. They were waiting for further instructions from the BCCI back home, but they even went as far as threatening to abandon the tour. They demanded that Steve Bucknor never umpire a Test again. The veteran West Indian had endured a tough Test, but his career deserved more respect than that.

Any umpire or referee can have a bad day at the office, but Bucknor had served with distinction and character for years. He was caught in the emotional cross-fire that had already seen the spills from off the field overshadow the thrills on it, sadly. The irony, of course, is that India were the last superpower that finally agreed to utilise the Decision Review System, which sought to eliminate the howler decisions from the game. Only recently have they come around to having faith in the system.

India moved on to Adelaide for the appeal, and legend has it that they had a private jet on standby, in case the appeal went against them, too. The appeal, chaired by Judge Hanson from New Zealand, decreed that the matter was a re-hearing, and cast aside what had happened in the initial proceedings, deep into the Sydney night.

All our running around, preparing a venue for the hearing, and then the hours and hours of deliberation, had suddenly been reduced to being a footnote. It had been one of the most stressful nights of my life, and I distinctly remember climbing into bed just as the sun was about to come up.

By the time the hearing came around, all that work seemed to be for naught. I couldn't understand that at all, and was further mystified when Tendulkar suddenly emerged as the key witness. Where was this testimony when it was originally asked for? Of course, with this new evidence coming to the fore, Judge Hanson downgraded Harbhajan's charge from racial abuse to one of verbal abuse. Of course, he belatedly admitted that his verdict would have been very different if he had been put in the full picture about Harbhajan's previous misdemeanours.

I couldn't quite believe it, but moved on to the final Test, already knowing that this series would be my last as a Test match referee. It must be said that the Indian team never behaved in any untoward manner towards me in that final Test. They were cordial, and I certainly didn't feel any sort of bad blood. The sting in the tail was yet to hit me, though, as the BCCI made it very clear to me that I was persona non grata in their eyes after the whole episode.

The ICC have age guidelines for umpires and for match referees, and I was just about at the cut-off point. I knew that there was a very good chance that the series between Australia and India would be my final bow, but I had not banked on finishing off in the circumstances that I did.

The whole 'Monkeygate' scandal started to make sense to me in the months and years that followed, as I learnt that Cricket Australia had leant heavily on the players to take the racism allegation away, and instead make it a matter of abuse. The looming threat of India pulling out of the tour would have major repercussions for Cricket Australia, and a potential lawsuit from the big broadcasters.

That, to me, was incredible. How a national board could try to convince senior players to downgrade an allegation as serious as racial abuse, in order to maintain ties with another board was mind-boggling, but it was the first time I realised just how much of a stronghold India had on the game. I had always known they were the biggest market in terms of fans and television money, but I obviously had no real grasp of how much power they exerted, even over traditional powers like Australia.

'I think Cricket Australia was intimidated by the Indian Cricket Board,' Symonds was later quoted as saying on the Cricinfo website.

Even to me, it was quite illuminating to see the lengths Cricket Australia went towards appeasing the Indian team and management, when it was apparent that it was an Australian player that had been wronged.

Former captain, Allan Border, was also outspoken on the matter, in his book, *Cricket As I See it*. Border was a board member at the time, and he said 'the matter never sat well' with him. He felt that Cricket Australia let Symonds down, and the player was never the same afterwards. Border also criticised the fact that Cricket Australia and the ICC encouraged players to report abuse, and then did nothing when those reports came forward.

Incredibly, Andrew Symonds became the fall guy in a sense. I certainly didn't think he was an angel, but he was made to appear as if he wasn't telling the truth.

'The thing, I think, that was grinding on me the most was the lying. Because the allegation was that this hadn't happened, and it had. Then the lies started, and then it became political. The captain (Ricky Ponting) was made to look like a fool, and that should never have happened, and the other players too. If truth, honesty and common sense had prevailed, then there'd have been a punishment for the player. It would have been dealt with and there would be a precedent for the future,' he said in the same Cricinfo interview.

It certainly would have set a precedent, and if the whole matter had been laid out in the open at the initial hearing, then things would have been wholly different.

It seemed that the episode was the beginning of the end for Symonds as an international cricketer, and he retired not too long after that. I felt that the Monkeygate episode played a big role in that, and Ponting and Gilchrist later admitted that they, too, felt that Cricket Australia had let him down.

The reaction to the initial hearing made out as if I had called Harbhajan a racist, which was far from the truth. My job had been to look into an allegation of racial abuse, and he never did anything to defend himself in that regard. He left me with no option to even consider otherwise, but I certainly didn't label him as a racist.

The fallout from that whole Monkeygate scandal was very damaging for me, personally. In India, where I have so many great memories, I became public enemy number one. I had been awarded an honorary life membership at the prestigious Cricket Club of India, in the 90s. I have since tried to contact the club, to confirm that I am still a member. There was no response. When a mate of mine went over to India, I asked him to enquire about my membership, but they told him that they had no record of me being a member, which I found quite bizarre.

Worse was to follow for the 2009 IPL, which was held in South Africa, due to the elections in India at the same time. I had been sent a contract to sign to be a match referee, and that was awaiting the accompanying signature of Lalit Modi.

I had even been sent the itinerary for the whole tournament, and I was looking forward to being involved. And then, just like that, the plug was pulled and there was absolutely no explanation.

It didn't take long to figure that there must have been an eyebrow raised at MJ Procter being match referee after everything that had happened in January 2008.

The entire episode left a very bad aftertaste, and I for one was not happy with the brush that I was tarred with. I still insist that I was just doing my job at the end of that chaotic New Year Test at the SCG, and I have been paying a silent price ever since.

Chapter 7

The walk-offs

I HAVE BEEN involved in two walk-offs in my cricket career. The first one, when I was still a player, was down to political reasons, and one that we all felt we had to do, to at least make our stance known on a bigger scale.

Back in the late 60s, as the apartheid regime took hold and isolated us from the rest of the world, there was not too much we could do about it. But, as players, we felt very strongly that we had to be seen to be making some sort of statement about what we saw as racial discrimination.

England were due to tour South Africa in 1968/69. With Basil D'Oliveira being a player of mixed race, there was a lot of talk about whether Basil would be selected, given the political climate in South Africa. I followed this very closely, because I had got to know Basil fairly well, and had played against him in county cricket that year. A lot of us were very happy when 'Dolly' scored 158 in the final Test of the Ashes in 1968, which was the last Test before the squad to tour South Africa was to be announced. He also took a vital wicket, to secure a victory for England in the same match. We all assumed he would be part of the tour.

So it was a shock to all of us when his name was not in the touring party, and it was seen to be due to political reasons. It rightly caused a huge outcry all over the world. Fate wouldn't allow the matter to die quietly though, and Tom Cartwright, a bowler, injured his shoulder just weeks after the announcement. England chose D'Oliveira as his replacement which might not make much cricket sense.

You had a bowler being replaced by a top-order batsman, but there was a lot more going on, of course. I think the England selectors saw Cartwright's injury as a blessing in disguise, and picked 'Dolly', who should have been in the team in the first place. They picked him, knowing that he deserved to be there, and then left the ball squarely in the South African government's court. The then prime minister of South Africa, John Vorster, labelled the team as not being part of the MCC, but that of an anti-apartheid movement, and the tour was cancelled. It was, we knew, the beginning of the end for South Africa in international cricket.

At the end of the 1970/71 season, there was a match organised by South African Sport and Recreation, between Transvaal – the Currie Cup champions – and the Rest of South Africa, as part of the South African Games. On the team sheets, it was the proverbial who's who of South African cricket. Barry Richards, a young Clive Rice, Vince van der Bijl, Graeme and Peter Pollock, Denis Lindsay – we were all there. We had met prior to the match, and decided that we needed to make a statement to the world about what we thought of politics interfering with the game we all loved.

A couple of days prior to the match taking place, the South African Cricket Association had told the government of their intention to include two non-white cricketers in the squad to tour Australia, but the government said there was no way that would happen.

I remember having dinner with Denis Lindsay and the Pollock brothers, where we discussed what we would do to show our support for the South African Cricket Association, and we knew that we had the backing of nearly all the players on both teams. By extension, we also felt that we were standing for the majority of the cricket players in the Currie Cup.

We had discussed not playing at all, and had virtually made up our minds not to play. The late Charles Fortune, a doyen of South African sports journalism, was in the same dining room. I knew Charles quite well, as he commentated on cricket, and I had also seen him at tennis tournaments when my wife Maryna was still playing. We decided that I should approach him for some advice, as this was a very loaded statement that we were about to make to the world.

I told Charles of our intentions, and he gave it some thought. He then suggested that we should play the game, but have the walk-off after the first ball. His reasoning was that such an action would have the same effect as not playing at all, but we would have more people on our side. Thousands of tickets had already been sold, so we had a captive audience. If we then made our statement, it would have a far bigger impact.

I went back to the table, and told the rest of the guys what Charles had suggested. Peter Pollock, who was the senior pro amongst us – and a journalist himself – and essentially our spokesman, wrote a statement which we all agreed upon. It was this statement that we read to the media, when we staged the walk-off.

'We fully support the South African Cricket Association's application to invite non-whites to tour Australia, if they are good enough. And further, subscribe to merit being the only criteria on the cricket field.'

I had run in to bowl to Barry Richards, who was opening the batting for Transvaal. They had won the toss and elected to bat. The plan was to bowl the first ball, and then walk off the field.

Barry, an avid collector of runs, still managed to squeeze out a single in the circumstances – and he would later quip that he was still getting paid by the run in his contract!

Once we walked off, we handed over the statement to the South African Cricket Association, stating that we fully supported the inclusion of two non-white players to tour Australia. The match then continued, and it would eventually end in a draw.

But, the point of the exercise was for us as players to be seen – on the only platform that we had – to be strongly against racial discrimination. I can't say how big an impact it made, but I was proud to be associated with a group of players that understood that there were wider implications at play, all around us.

We couldn't change our circumstances, but we also couldn't stand by silently and ignore what was going on in our own country. I have always maintained that sport and politics are a dangerous mix, and nothing in my career has ever changed that assessment.

The second walk-off, decades later, followed an altercation between the Pakistan team and Australian umpire Darrell Hair on 20 August 2006 at The Oval. It was an astonishing day, and the build-up to that dramatic conclusion had started in earnest right from the first match of the series.

Ranjan Madugalle had been the match referee in the first three Test matches, and he would be the first to admit that things had not gone as smoothly as they could have. It was a bizarre arrangement, as Ranjan had the majority of the Tests, and then I was left with the final Test, and then the one-day series. His report had suggested that there wasn't much harmony between Darrell Hair and the Pakistan players, and there had also been a few issues with Darrell and some Pakistan spectators in the third Test at Leeds.

There had already been a fair amount of discussion about ball-tampering, and Hair was actively on the lookout for it. While Pakistan had a reputation for being very skilled in the art of reverse-swing bowling, it had long been suggested in some quarters that they were ball-tampering.

Trying to tamper with the ball in the modern era was very difficult, of course, as there are cameras everywhere. They lock in on anything that even looks vaguely suspicious, and the ball is regularly inspected by the on-field umpires. But, for one reason or another, the insinuation was in the atmosphere, and Pakistan hadn't taken too kindly to it. It was a situation that was brewing all the time, and we were trying to calm things down. Test matches are tense as it is, without the sideshow of accusations of cheating. It was just my luck, of course, that the real drama kicked off once I was in the hot seat. Darrell had already come to see me at the end of the England first innings.

'What do you think about this ball?' he had asked me provocatively.

I didn't see anything too untoward with the ball, and that was that. On that fourth morning, I had gone to see the two coaches, Duncan Fletcher and Bob Woolmer, before play. I felt it was my job as match referee to get the sides to gel as much as possible, and I knew both Bob and Duncan very well. As I walked back to the umpires' rooms, I ran into Darrell. For some reason, it occurred to me to ask him about our conversation about the ball.

I asked him if anything would come of him having asked me to look at the condition earlier in the match.

To this day, I will always remember Darrell's words.

'The match will take its course,' he declared.

The match certainly did take a dramatic course as, midway through the day's play, the umpires decided to punish Pakistan for altering the state of the ball. Darrell showed the scorers that he was awarding five runs to the batting side, and he called for a change of ball.

Pakistan, naturally, were apoplectic. Play continued, in strained circumstances, and then there was a premature halt, due to drizzle and bad light, which forced an early tea. Bob Woolmer and Waqar Younis came straight to my rooms during the break, and asked what on earth was going on.

Bob Woolmer was fuming, and he suggested that we might struggle to convince his team to get back on the field. They were furious about the whole thing, and I suppose they were relating it to everything that had gone on during the entire series.

I suddenly realised that we may not get both teams back on the park in time for that. England's batsmen were already on the stairs, not sure whether to go all the way down, or to go back in the dressing room.

The rest of the England players were on the balcony, while the crowd could sense that something was amiss. The umpires made their way out to the middle at the right time, but there was no fielding side walking out behind them.

Pakistan were still in their dressing room, and they didn't sound too keen to come out, because they felt that they were being unfairly targeted. What had been a feisty contest between two proud teams had now escalated into an international incident.

The television producers were trying to understand what was going on, and I was still trying to pacify the Pakistan team in their dressing room. Zaheer Abbas, who I had played with at Gloucestershire, was the team manager, and I had been trying to call him before getting to the dressing room. When I did get to him, I was trying to assure them that this matter would be dealt with accordingly after the game, which we needed to get on with first. While I was dealing with all that, I could suddenly hear a chorus of boos from the middle, and figured something else had happened.

England appeared confused, but Darrell then told them that Pakistan had failed to get back on the field in time, on two occasions, and the umpires considered their actions as a sign of a forfeit.

Of course, under the rules, Pakistan had transgressed. A bit of common sense suggested that they were feeling picked on, and England seemed to understand that much, at least. These were not usual circumstances, and England were still keen to continue with the match.

Pakistan, having failed to show up when the 20-minute tea break ended, eventually went down the stairs on to the field. The crowd sort of cheered, but there was still confusion. Bob Woolmer had finally got to his senior players, especially skipper Inzamam-ul-Haq, and reasoned that this could be sorted out in a different way, but to forfeit the match would cause an international outrage.

I still hadn't been officially informed that the match had been called off. When I went back to the umpires' rooms, Darrell was standing there, wearing a large towel. I asked him what was going on, and he replied matter-of-factly.

'The match has been called off.'

I had sort of figured that much, but it was nice to finally have word from the umpires, as the match referee.

In over 1,000 Test matches played before that day, none had ever ended in those circumstances. Some of Darrell's actions had clearly rubbed the Pakistan team up the wrong way, and he himself seemed to be almost working on an agenda.

Again, the severity of the situation saw to it that there was an ICC rule change after the events at The Oval. Umpires could no longer call off a match without prior consultation with and the consent of the match referee.

It was a messy, embarrassing way to end a Test match for everyone else concerned, and the match was abandoned just like that. Darrell was far from done, however. Soon after the game, he offered his resignation to the ICC, even though his contract still had another 18 months or so to run. He wasn't going to walk away with nothing, of course. He wanted a non-negotiable, one-off payment of $500,000, to cover the loss of earnings over that period, and the two years after that, when he anticipated to still be good enough to be on the Elite Umpires' Panel.

That payment was supposedly to be kept private between the ICC and Hair, but these things always find a way to come out. He insisted that there had been negotiations that had been ongoing with the ICC prior to the revelations, but he would eventually be banned from officiating before the end of that year.

Darrell Hair was an excellent umpire, but he tended to be heavy-handed when he had a hunch on something. As an umpire, I have always thought that one of the responsibilities of the job is to remain impartial at all times, emotionally removed from the events on the field. I am not so sure that Darrell always managed to remove himself in that manner, and it led to some very tense moments over the course of his career.

I had first encountered Darrell during South Africa's compelling tour of 1994, when I was the South African coach. The first Test in Melbourne had been a washout, and then we had that terrific, five-run victory in Sydney, thanks to a magical spell by Fanie de Villiers.

Shane Warne, turning it a mile, took 12 wickets in the match, but still ended up on the losing side. Our final day miracle owed a lot to the efforts of Jonty Rhodes and Allan Donald with the bat, when they added 36 for the final wicket. It might not sound like a lot, but it allowed us to set the Aussies 117 to win, and take the match into the fifth morning.

Hansie Cronje was stand-in captain on that final morning, due to Kepler Wessels breaking a finger. Hansie was in inspired form that day, and his brilliant run-out of Warne from the boundary was just as crucial to our cause.

Damien Martyn, a wonderfully fluent batsman in his later years, simply froze at the crease on that final morning, and he was dropped for a long time afterwards. On the field, the team had kept reminding the batsmen how Australia tended to struggle chasing low totals, and I think that really got to Martyn.

Donald had bowled with pace up front, but Fanie was the hero, with a sensational spell of swing bowling. He ended up with figures of 6-43, and he fittingly took the final wicket. It had been a wonderful fightback, against the odds, and that whole match was a lesson in never giving up. Fanie, with the ball, and Jonty with the bat, had simply dug in and refused to give up the ghost.

On the back of the miracle in Sydney, we felt that the series was within our grasp, and went to Adelaide for the third Test in especially good spirits. What followed was a match where the lbw decision count was skewed 7-1, against us. Peter Kirsten, who was at the non-striker's end for several of those leg-before decisions from Hair, had a very animated discussion with the umpire about them.

Of course, Peter was also eventually dismissed leg-before, and he blew his top. He was fined 40% of his match fee for dissent, and he was fuming at what he saw as terrible umpiring. We were very disappointed, too, and that match left a very bitter taste in the mouth. This was long before the days of the DRS system, so a few of the guys copped what looked to be rough decisions.

The umpires were staying in the same hotel as us, and when we got back to the hotel that day, there was a clutch of South African fans in the foyer, still steaming about Darrell Hair's performance. I was sure they knew that he was staying in the same hotel, but I went over to pacify them, and reminded them that the game wasn't over.

I am quite certain that they were ready to give Darrell a piece of their mind, and things could have become quite heated. We ultimately lost that final Test match by 191 runs, but Fanie again dug in. Coming in as nightwatchman, he made a defiant 30 in a vigil with Peter Kirsten in the second innings. Fanie was a wonderful character, and a great guy to have in the team, but even his indefatigable spirit couldn't save that Test for us.

Looking back on that final Test, and then on to some of the challenges that have followed Darrell Hair in his career, it is uncanny how controversy seems to follow certain figures in the game. Darrell had huge drama with Sri Lankan spinner Muttiah Muralitharan, too, calling him for no-balls several times, and he has remained a very outspoken figure on the state of the game, especially since retiring as an international umpire.

Chapter 8

The time of my life

MY LIFE changed forever when Gloucestershire became part of my cricketing CV. What made it even more remarkable was that I was initially plucked from South Africa on the back of a recommendation from senior South African players like Jackie McGlew, who had earmarked Barry Richards and I as talents when fate came knocking.

David Allen, who played for Gloucestershire, had come on tour to South Africa in 1963/64 with the MCC, and the county had asked him to try and find some young talents to perhaps bring over. A few of the South African senior players suggested that Barry and I were the best bet, having excelled in the schools ranks, and made the South African Schools XI.

And so, Barry and I were invited to England in the 1965 season, to see if we could adapt and play in a new environment. We could only play for the second XI, but it was obviously very exciting, and we both went on to enjoy a very decent summer there. We actually won the second XI championship that year. It was great playing against the other teams around the country and playing opposite other famous cricket guys.

Funnily enough, we both played against the South Africans, as they were touring there, and Gloucestershire were one of their warm-up matches. It was my debut in first-class cricket. Though Jackie McGlew and company had put in a good word for us, that South African team that we came up against certainly didn't take it easy when Barry and I were batting together in the middle. We came together at 62 for 4, and we put on 116. Barry made 59, and I made the top score of 69, in a total of 270. It was tough, uncompromising, but we loved every second of it, because we were proving ourselves against men who would eventually become our team-mates in national colours. Unfortunately, it rained for the next two days, so there was no more play!

Another game that I remember fondly was against the touring Indian Test side, though that was later down the line. In that side, alongside the likes of Sunil Gavaskar, was one Chetan Chauhan, who was an opening batsman. India batted first, and declared at 337 for 5. I then declared at 254 for 7, giving them a lead of 83. We then bowled India out for 117, and I returned figures of 7-13 in 15.3 overs. Zaheer and I were there at the end to knock off the winning runs, and we won by a very satisfying seven wickets. Chetan, of course, was to go on to become the team manager, and was central in the 'Monkeygate' scandal of 2008. Funnily enough, we never did get the time to sit over a cup of tea and reminisce about that game, but the coincidence is just another reminder of how small and far-reaching this great game of ours is.

At the end of that season obviously, Gloucestershire wanted us to come back, but the regulation then was that you had to spend at least two years in the county. You were allowed out for three months or four months, but obviously, we were never going to reside in Gloucestershire and qualify to play for Gloucestershire that way because we had careers back home. So, we obviously went back home and nothing more became of it until before the 1968 season in England. There was a new regulation brought forward, that said each county could have one overseas player without having to qualify. And so, from 1968, I went to Gloucestershire and Barry went to Hampshire.

My first contract was for £1,750 for the season, and then they sorted out all the board and lodging. I just wanted to get on the park and play again in Gloucestershire colours. I was really proud when I became captain in 1977, which was a great year for us, as we won the Benson and Hedges Cup Final, and almost won the county championship, too.

It was a huge change in living, coming from South Africa to going to another country, although I had obviously been to Bristol in 1965. I had also been in England in 1963, when I toured with the South African Schools, so it wasn't all new to me. I wasn't married then, so being single meant I wasn't too concerned about much other than cricket. That made settling into life there a little easier, just being on my own.

The weather was the real crunch for me, though. I couldn't believe just how cold it was. I remember Barry and I sort of joking that we should tell them our fielding positions were fine leg and third man, because we didn't want to get too near where the ball would come flying at a hundred miles an hour! We obviously ended up in the slip cordon, anyway, but I think the weather was the hardest aspect to get used to. The pitches were also different, but you adapt to that. It didn't take too long either, and in fact my maiden county hundred came in 1968. It also happened to be against Barry's Hampshire. It was early days in the season, towards the end of May. We were sent in to bat by Hampshire and they had three international bowlers in their attack. When I came in, batting number five, we were already 23 for 3, which then became 43 for 4, then 49 for 5! I ended up getting 101, and we were bowled out for 251.

Hampshire got 221, and then bowled us out for very little, to win quite comfortably. I remember the wicket seaming around a fair amount but, as far as I was concerned, it was a great start.

But, the cold was still taking some getting used to. Even in later years, when we had people round for dinner with Maryna, we joked that we had to put the white wine outside to get cold! Early in the season, it was really, really hard. I think the guys used to have hand warmers and things like that. Playing in that weather was really the toughest part.

There is a lot of importance attached to being a county cap in England, and I didn't initially recognise the significance. Arthur Milton, who was captain, gave me my county cap, and I just sort of took it in my stride. It was only later that I realised the significance, and being a capped player meant you really were part of the first team. Once you are capped, it is sort of a rough guideline to when you may eventually get a benefit year, and things like that.

I settled in nicely in Bristol, and I figured pretty quickly that international cricket was going to be out of the window for us. Some guys still held hope, but you could see the situation getting worse. So I just concentrated on playing for Gloucestershire and doing the best I could, whether it was for them, or for Rhodesia, or Natal.

I never felt in any way ostracised at all being South African as far as the actual cricket was concerned. In fact, when I was captain of Gloucestershire, Ken Graveney was chairman, and the famous commentator, John Arlott, invited both of us over to his house for dinner.

We were playing at Southampton and Ken happened to be staying over and watching the cricket. John was a huge wine connoisseur, and he could really lay on a spread. We had a fantastic evening, talking about various topics. He was a fascinating man, with a lot of insights on a range of topics, and he was also very much against the apartheid system, and had been a strong advocate for Basil D'Oliviera and, in fact, was instrumental in getting Dolly to come and play in England. It was an honour to be invited like that, and it was a real highlight for me.

I also remember when Gloucestershire played Middlesex in 1980, which was Vince van der Bijl's only season playing for them. Mike Brearley was the captain and they had a number of international players in their team, including Wayne Daniel, the West Indies fast bowler. Middlesex got 220 or so in the first innings, and then rolled us for just 109. Vince took four and Wayne Daniel helped himself to five wickets. Then, in the second innings, Brearley declared their second innings after they passed 150, setting us 270-odd to win. We ended up getting there, and I scored 134 not out. As I recall, we won with something like half an hour to spare. Brearley had obviously planned on either bowling us out, or on us not having enough time to get the runs, but we just went for it. That was a very satisfying win, especially as we had been so far behind after the first innings. It was always nice to get one over Brearley, who was a brilliant tactician – and someone many still insist was England's best ever post-war captain. It was a personal honour to hear Mike name me as one of his favourite captains in the game.

1977 was obviously a massive year for Gloucestershire cricket, and sometimes our run to the final is overlooked, because the game that is most remembered is obviously the final. But the run that got us there was pretty special, too.

In the quarter-finals, we played Middlesex and made 194 for 7. In those days, we played 55 overs per side. 194 was below par, but we managed to bowl them out for 176. I got 3-15 from 9.1 overs.

The semi-final against Hampshire was obviously a hugely important game for us. The weather was fantastic at Southampton, and we played on a very good pitch, with a very fast outfield. To top it off, it was quite a smallish ground. We were about 100-odd for 1 at one stage, but we then had an almighty collapse and we were bowled out for 180. So, we had to defend that under-par total against a line-up that included Barry Richards and Gordon Greenidge opening the batting. We knew from the start that we would be up against it, and we were going to have to play out of our skins to get anything out of the game. I had been struggling to get going, and it was most peculiar because when I was bowling over the wicket, it didn't seem to swing much. I always tried different things to see if they could work, so I went around the wicket. Bizarrely, it swung much more from around the wicket than it did over the wicket. Considering the angle I was bowling with, it was hugely surprising to get the ball to come back in that much.

In my third over, I somehow turned the match on its head! I got Barry out first, and then suddenly got three more wickets, to make it four in five balls! Suddenly, from 19 for 1, Hampshire crashed to 19 for 5! I was just concentrating on hitting the right length, and I just couldn't miss. That was the catalyst for our victory, and the run that ultimately led us to the cup win in the final. We eventually bowled out Hampshire for 173, and beat them by a handful of runs to go through to the semis. I ended with figures of 6-13 in 11 overs, and it was really one of my most enjoyable spells. I felt in wonderful rhythm that season, and the ball came out fantastically right through our cup run.

A semi-final is probably the hardest game to lose, because you miss out in at least taking part in a final. In that game, I felt that my most important moment was not so much the wickets up front, but rather the penultimate over, when Hampshire still needed 12 to win. Andy Roberts, the West Indian fast bowler, was still batting, and he was a dangerous hitter. He certainly wasn't an out and out tail-ender, and I looked at that penultimate over as the key in winning the match. If they hit a couple of boundaries, then all the pressure would go away, and they would cruise home. In that particular over, I managed to go for just one run, and also got a vital wicket. So, they needed ten off the last over, and they only got a couple. Brian Brain bowled the last over, and he got Andy Roberts out. We won a very tight match by seven runs, and we were obviously chuffed to have held our nerve in that fashion.

The final itself was a big occasion. The match at Lord's is sold out months before, so you couldn't even buy tickets. It was certainly a big deal. That match really kick-started a love affair with 'HQ', as some referred to Lord's. Throughout my playing career, I loved going there, because it was always a huge occasion. Even when I went back beyond my playing days, as director of cricket at Northamptonshire – when we won a final there, with Curtly Ambrose in the side – and then, famously, with the South African side of 1994, it was always special. I suppose it helped that I usually ended up on the right side of the result, as we did in 1994, and we got into a bit of trouble for proudly flying the South African flag from the balcony. The entire team was buzzing for that match, so you couldn't blame them for showing a bit of exuberance when we won South Africa's first match back at Lord's in decades.

Back in that 1977 final, we chose to bat on a good wicket and we knew we had to get a good start. Everyone got runs for us, but the highlights were Andy Stovald and Zaheer Abbas making a pair of 70s. We made 237 for 6 in the 55 overs, after a good start had taken us to 80-odd for 1, and then 150-odd for 2. I got 25, and we maintained a steady run-rate right through our innings. 237 was probably just about par, but we knew that we would have to bowl and field very well. That was exactly what we did. Up front we bowled really tight, and that pressure led to a couple of early wickets. I bowled a spell of seven overs up front, and chipped in with 1-15. Brian Brain, at the other end, ended up bowling 7.3 overs, and registering figures of 3-9. That's really where we won the game, by pegging them back to 24 for 3. The overs that Kent took, trying to get a grip on the chase again, is what ultimately lost them the game, I thought. They had Bob Woolmer, Asif Iqbal, Bernard Julien, John Sheppard, Alan Knott, and deadly Derek

Underwood in their side, so they were certainly no mugs. We bowled them out for 173 in the 47th over, to wrap up a quality team performance.

We spent the night in London, and then drove back to Bristol the next morning. Naturally, the celebrations continued there, and we went to what was regarded as the team pub. They always looked after us, and quite a few fans used to frequent the place. We tended to look after the places that looked after us, and we had a most memorable evening toasting our success.

That season could have been even more memorable for us. We had been going pretty nicely in the championship, and we got ourselves into a position where we had a chance of securing a unique double, going into the final round. If we won we would have won the county championship, or at least shared it. The whole run up to that last game was very exciting, because we knew we were close to something very special, having already won the Benson and Hedges. Again, it was against Hampshire. I hadn't gotten many runs that season actually, and I was desperate to contribute now, when the team needed it most. We batted first, and we ended on a disappointing 223. I had come in at 28 for 3, and I ended up getting 100. In fact, that was my only first-class hundred for the season. Better late than never, I suppose.

At that time of year, the wicket was always going to turn a little bit. Hampshire replied with 229, and I bowled off-breaks for most of the innings, putting in a shift of 39 overs, 6-68. In the second dig, we went along pretty well, but were bowled out for 276. I added 57 to that first innings century. It is perhaps a weird thing to say now, but I think the wicket changed after our innings. It certainly didn't turn on the third day as much as it had on the first or second day. It was a bit flatter, and I think I erred in captaincy that game. I kept bowling the spinners for too long, when I may have been better served going back to seamers a bit earlier. I remember bringing Brian Brain back, and he immediately got a couple of wickets. It was too little, too late, and we ended up losing quite convincingly, by six wickets. It was a very sad way to end a fantastic season, but that is how the game goes, sometimes. You can't win them all.

The other trophy that we won was in 1973, in the Gillette Cup. In the final, I got 94 and was out trying to hit a six. I had got a hundred in a tight semi-final win over Worcestershire. In keeping up with the reputation that I generally scored my runs when the chips were down, I got to the crease when we were 20 for 3 in that final.

That was against Tony Greig's Sussex side. They had Greigy and John Snow and I think we were the underdogs there. Those were great times. Fantastic. Again, we spent the night in London and then got back to Gloucester the next day. We got welcomed wherever we went. Everyone in Bristol was delighted about the whole thing. We did a bus parade with the trophy – not quite as big as the footballers, that is for sure. But it was a nice touch.

We actually had a few players who were professional footballers, too. In those days, there was still a distinction between winter and summer sports. Arthur Milton, who was my first Gloucestershire captain, played England football and England cricket. Barry Meyer, an umpire who ended up living in South Africa, played for both Bristol City and Bristol Rovers, as well as Gloucestershire. Another guy, Harold Jarman who spent more time in our second side, also played for City and Rovers. You obviously couldn't do that now.

As I settled into my work at Gloucester, I would get enquiries from other counties at the end of every season, offering more money for me to move there. I considered myself a loyal guy, though, so it didn't even enter my mind. Gloucester were looking after me just fine, so I wouldn't even entertain them.

Things were going very well, though I remember one night where I strayed out of hand as captain. My brother Anton came over and we hadn't had much contact, because he had been in Rhodesia just before I went there. He has always been into his horses, and he had come over to buy a stallion race horse. In those times in Rhodesia, foreign currency was near impossible to get hold of. But the guy whose stud he was looking after had accumulated something like £10,000, to buy a stallion. So Anton came over when he was negotiating with the guy at Newmarket, and he borrowed 200 quid from me to top up the kitty. Anton came and stayed with us while he negotiated the deal, which happened to be on the Saturday of a game we were playing against Somerset.

Brian Rose was captain of Somerset, Dickie Bird was one of the umpires, and it was one of those overcast, drizzly days in Bristol. It really looked as though we would struggle to play if there was any sort of rain, as there was no sun to dry the pitch out. The umpires were supposed to inspect the pitch at midday, and I remember me saying to Dickie that they should just make a decision because obviously we were not going to play. The day was eventually abandoned early, and we had an early lunch. We still had a Sunday League one-day match to play the next day.

There was racing at Bath, so a friend of mine called Dave Drinkwater invited my brother, Anton's farrier and I to go. So, the four of us went to the racing at Bath. Dave and I spent most of the time in the pub, while Anton and the farrier spent most of the time looking at the horses. It got to the last race, and we hadn't backed any winners. So, I said to Dave that he should be finding the winners because he was the host, and that's the way it works. But obviously, it doesn't work like that here, I chirped! I then went outside and had a look at the horses on the betting board, and there were 12 horses in the field. There were four horses in the betting and the rest were priced very long. I made a note of the four and I went back into the pub with my mate and came up with a bet.

'Listen, we put £50 in, and I'll pick four horses, and you can have the rest. Then, whoever loses puts 50 quid in the drinks kitty.' Naturally, I picked the four that were in the betting! This was all after a few drinks, so, things were a bit blurred. So, obviously one of these four won, and there was now an extra 50 quid in the kitty. We had to spend that money, so we left the bar very late! In fact, we might have even helped them close up!

We then moved on to another pub, owned by a mate of mine called Tom Hennessy. He was a fantastic publican and worked hard. He used to look after us. All this time, we were supposed to be going out to dinner, and my brother was also supposed to be going out to dinner with friends, as well. The one thing I did remember to do just before I left the cricket ground was to ask David Shepherd to give me a ring in the morning, if we were going to play. I don't know what compelled me to say that to Shep, but it was just as well. Play only started at 2pm, anyway, so there was no real reason to need Shep to be an alarm!

After the pub, I eventually joined Maryna and the rest of the dinner party, which was hosted by our good friends, Carol and Tony Windows. Maryna left early, but I stayed on until about 4am, when I suddenly noticed that the sun was coming up! Despite that very obvious signal from Mother Nature, it still didn't register that we might actually play! My wife wasn't very happy when I did eventually get to bed, and quite rightly. I was then woken up with a call from Shep, saying that we are starting on time! I was in a bad way, and remember thinking that if I won the toss, for the first time in my life I may have to prioritise my own health. We ended up batting first, and I came in not feeling in very good health. We were about 40 for 2, and it was really hot now. I took guard and, on the first ball, I made a big mistake, which I don't normally do, anyway. I left the ball, and with my foot planted down the wicket, and my arms in the air, I overbalanced and fell straight on my face! I remember sheepishly looking at my boots, and I could hear this raucous laughter from the boundaries. My mates knew what was going on – and what had gone on the night before!

Anyway, I stuck around for a while, and got 30-odd. We were playing a 40-over game, and we got around 200. It was probably just below par. And I remember saying to the guys that we couldn't afford any extras. I said if we bowl and field well, we would win this game. I took the first over. Dickie Bird was standing at my end and it swung down the leg side. Wide ball. I wasn't too bothered, and I got back to my mark. The next one started outside off stump, but didn't swing at all. In fact, it was too far outside off stump, and was another wide. So now I start panicking a bit. So I went around the wicket. But now, around the wicket, you don't know how far the ball is going to swing or not. So, I ran up, held the ball to try and swing it, started it around off stump, and it swung way down the leg side again, for another wide.

So now, they're chasing 200, they've got three runs on the board and they haven't started the innings yet! Next ball, I very gingerly idled up to the wicket across the seam and got it down the other end. Fortunately, I got away with it, and we somehow ended up winning by about five or six runs.

I had left the last over of the match to Brian, as I didn't fancy myself bowling. As we were coming off the field, I saw Ken Graveney in the crowd. He never missed a beat.

'Well then, captain. It is a good job you won the game, otherwise we might have had to find a new skipper!'

I don't know whether he meant that seriously or it was a bit tongue in cheek, but he had obviously heard what had been going on. Actually, now that I think of it, I am not so sure that Anton ever paid me back the 200 quid! The compound interest on that, after 30-odd years, would be most interesting!

We had some amazing times back then, but we also had some interesting challenges along the way. I used to get a sponsored car, and one year, we were driving back to Bristol from a match at Loughborough. We stopped to fill up the tank, and in England, you fill your own petrol, as there are no petrol attendants. So, I just took a nozzle and started filling the car up. As it turned out, I put diesel in a petrol car. So, we didn't get too far. We went about 20 metres and boom, the car stops.

We had to find transport all the way back to Bristol, and the company who lent me the car weren't very happy, because you have got to drain the whole petrol tank. I learnt from that mistake, and always made sure to check.

One of my favourite memories from Gloucester was playing a crazy game of single-wicket rugby against the gregarious David Green, my best mate in the team, in 1968. We were playing against Warwickshire, at Coventry, and we had a day off on the Sunday, as was the custom back then. We had already marked the previous evening by cutting loose at an event for Tom Cartwright's benefit year, so we were feeling rather tender the next morning.

David and I decided that the best way to get rid of the hangover was to get back on the sauce, and so off we went to Coventry, in search of a few pints. Over the course of those pints, we got to talking about rugby, and thus began a rather heated argument. The Springboks, at the time, were the dominant force in world rugby, and I took great delight in reminding David how they were smashing everyone who stood in their way.

He was never going to take that lying down, and soon enquired about my own set of rugby skills. Feeling as confident as ever, I regaled him with how cricket had got in the way of a most promising rugby career, explaining how I used pace, good hands and an eye for the gap to devastating effect.

The lager was still flowing, and David felt the need to declare his own prowess with the oval ball, going on about how he was a lethal tackler, and had one of those engines that went on forever on the field. We were really getting fired up, and we then decided that the best way to settle this matter was to play against each other, back at our hotel.

We were dressed quite smartly, as you did on Sundays, but this was no time to be going back upstairs for a change of clothes. We simply took off our jackets, and rolled up the sleeves on our shirts. Off came the shoes, and we marked out a field of sorts on the hotel lawns. The other guests, no doubt still digesting Sunday lunch, looked on with curiosity, as these two sportsmen carried on like schoolboys on the grass.

Already several pints down, the going was really tough! I had planned on using pace to get around David, but that is easier said than done after a few ales. David was less subtle, and simply tried to run straight over me. The result was several crunching tackles from both of us, and a sapping of the enthusiasm.

Thankfully, our senior pro in the team, John Mortimore, had heard the commotion, and had become a slightly concerned spectator. After all, we still had a game to play the next day, where I would probably be required to bat and bowl! After I had cut in on a run, and my knee had clattered into David's head, John demanded that we cut it out.

We were only too relieved to call a truce, and shook on it, with David still rubbing the lump on his head. As we came back to our senses, I was mortified to see the state of my trousers! They were part of my favourite silver-grey suit, but our exertions on the 'rugby field' had just about ruined them, with grass and mud stains everywhere! Looking back on it in later years, that rugby duel with David was completely bonkers, and would have required some explaining if one of us couldn't take the field the next day. To be honest, though, it was terrific fun while it lasted, and a great way to blow off some Sunday steam. As they say, all's well that ends well!

I also had a completely bizarre incident with the police in Bristol, with regards to a matter that ultimately involved human trafficking! I was renting out my house in Salisbury, now Harare, while I was in England for cricket, and I had a mate of mine who sorted out the tenants. The police took an interest in my house when the telephone bills escalated, with a lot of calls to Europe.

I was invited to sit down in an office, and still had no idea what was going on. An officer showed me a couple of photos, which were of my property in Salisbury. He asked me if I recognised them, and I said I did. He then showed me a few photos of people, and asked me if I knew them. I had no idea who they were, and after about 45 more minutes of probing, the boys in blue realised that I was not party to whatever it was that was going on! It was only later that I found out that the tenants were using the house as a base to carry out some serious human trafficking!

A much fonder memory from that time was one of the last games played at Bramall Lane, in Sheffield. It was Gloucestershire against Yorkshire, with Geoff Boycott as captain. Boycott had a strong side, with five or six international players. We bowled them out for 225, and I got four wickets. Then we made 270, and had a lead of 45. The pitch was acting up, and Yorkshire declared on 251 for 5, setting us a target of 200 in about 40 overs. I batted at four, and came in at 5 for 2, which soon became 11 for 3. In my mind, we have always got to go and try to get the runs if we can. If you lose, so be it. Boycott tried to bowl us out first, and then he could see we weren't really going for the runs. So he brought on John Hampshire, a part-time leg-spinner, to dangle the carrot. I told my partner to give it a go and see where we end up. Hampshire bowled three overs for 38. Suddenly, we were back in the game. That gift from Boycott gave us adrenalin, and I ended on 111 and we won by four wickets! It was even more satisfying because we had got one over Boycott. I get on well with Boycs, but everyone wanted to get Boycott out or beat him. I remember the Yorkshire lads moaning like hell about the fact that Boycott had declared, and then the wisdom of him bringing on a part-time leg-spinner!

I remember going through a purple patch in 1973, where I scored four centuries in 11 days. I then followed that up with a 94, and 2-20, in the final of the Gillette Cup. One of my favourite for Gloucestershire was at Essex in 1978, when I made 203. I was later told that it was generally regarded as the best innings seen on the ground since Wally Hammond's heyday, which was a very kind compliment.

There were others, like in '79, when I blitzed the fastest century of the season, in 57 minutes. I also smashed a hundred before lunch against Leicestershire, which I then followed up with a hat-trick. There was also a most satisfying outing against Worcestershire, at Cheltenham. We had bowled them out for 167, and I had taken 7-35. Overnight, we had a night-watchman in, and he went early the next day. I then came in and charged to a hundred before lunch! We made 338, and then bowled Worcestershire out for 136, and I took 6-38, to complete a rather successful outing.

A lot of people ask me about the 'Proctershire' nickname, and I found it all a bit embarrassing, really. I never felt as if I was carrying the team, and our victories were always down to more than one individual standing up. My stats and figures sometimes stood out, but I was just happy to be part of a very successful period in Gloucestershire's history. The county was wonderful to me, and I was proud to play a role in making history in the cups, and getting as close as we did in the championship.

Bristol became home, and I raised my family there. We had houses there, places that felt like home and were home. It was a bolt from the blue that got me to play for Gloucestershire, and I think both parties were very satisfied with the way it all worked out in the end.

To this day, I have fond friends in that part of the world, and the club remains very close to my heart.

Chapter 9

Growing up in the Currie Cup

W HEN I came back from my initial stint of second XI cricket in England in 1965, I knew that all I wanted to do was to be a professional cricketer. If there had been any lingering doubts, my summer in England, travelling the country, and pitting my wits against different players every single week, confirmed to me that I wanted to be a pro.

The only problem with that, of course, was that there was no professional cricket in South Africa at the time. Back in those days, first-class cricket was very limited, and we only played about six to eight matches a season. So, when they came around, those matches were pretty huge, because it was your one chance to prove yourself.

Before those matches, though, you had to play on the extremely competitive club circuit, which was the breeding ground for provincial colours. It saddens me when I see some of the great clubs of the past, real nurseries for some outstanding talent, diminish and pack it all in due to a shortage of players and general interest in the game.

When we were growing up, we knew that we had to quickly get into club cricket, because that was the stepping stone for higher honours. When I finished school, I started playing club cricket in Pietermaritzburg, for Collegians. I was working at Lambert's, which was a clothing store in the middle of town. It was my first full-time job, and I was a salesman, working Monday to Saturday morning.

I would get off if I was playing club cricket on the Saturday, as our league had two separate competitions. There was the limited-overs Sunday games, but there was also 'time cricket', which started on Saturday afternoon and went into Sunday.

I realised at that stage that if I was going to make it all the way to the top, it was likelier to be as a bowler, than as a batsman. With my action, it also became clear to me that I needed a long run-up to make the most of my bowling style. So there was a need to get fitter.

I would go down to Maritzburg College after work, and I would do some extra training on my own, using their rugby field markings. I would walk from the tryline to the 22m, then jog to the halfway line, before sprinting to the other side. I eventually worked up the stamina to get through 50–60 of those runs in each session, and those sessions were of great value to me as the season wore on.

The following season, I moved back to Durban and played for Rovers. The club scene was even more competitive. It was common for hundreds of people to turn up at the weekend to watch a game, and there was no quarter given on the field.

Away from the game, I became a partner in a sports firm, along with Reg Wright, Dan le Roux and Les Salton, all famous footballers in their time. We sold sports equipment, and we would all be in and around the shop during the week. They were good times, and it was my first taste of entrepreneurship. Once I headed over to county cricket, I sadly had to pull out of the business.

Going overseas at a young age had obviously put Barry and I even more in the spotlight, and there were definitely a few strong greetings that awaited the two new upstarts of South African cricket. Club cricket had always been regarded as the place where boys turned into men, and I revelled in the heat of battle, desperate to prove that I was ready to go up to the next level.

I still wasn't bowling at my absolute fastest, but I had bulked up in England, and had gained a few yards, as well as some very good knowledge of bowling on different surfaces. With Natal playing so infrequently, the club fixtures were the only place for anyone to stake a claim for the provincial team.

I had enjoyed a decent first half of the season, and earned my first-class call-up to the side. Those were the days of serious protocol in the game. When I was introduced to my captain, one Jackie McGlew, I had to refer to him as Mr McGlew, until I was told otherwise!

At 19, I was just thrilled to be finally in the changing room with the likes of McGlew, Roy McLean and Trevor Goddard, to name just a few. It was another step in the right direction, and playing with giants of South African cricket like Jackie McGlew inspired me even more.

We travelled up to Johannesburg to take on the Transvaal team on Boxing Day, at a Bullring that had the usual, boisterous festive season crowd. Though details of the match are a bit fuzzy, I do recall striking a knock of 70, and enjoying the thrill of playing on a hard, fast track, with an outfield that gave full value for your shots. When Transvaal came down to Durban for the return fixture in February, I was still enjoying some good form with the bat.

I have always been told that I made most of my really important runs when the team was under the cosh. I can't really explain the science behind it, except perhaps to say that I knew that the onus was on me – or else!

That game against Transvaal was the scene for my maiden first-class hundred. Transvaal had batted first, and notched a decent score, just short of 300. We had run into early trouble, and slumped to 19 for 4. Barry Richards was batting at three, but he had been injured and retired hurt pretty soon after going in.

Effectively, then, we were 19 for 5! I was in at seven, and it all happened in such a blur that I was still putting on my pads as I was walking out to the middle, to join a very concerned Berry Versfeld in the heat of battle.

Of course, I was a bit nervous, especially given what had just happened to our top order! What then followed was a partnership of 279. When I looked back on the numbers of that innings, I couldn't believe that I had somehow managed to have the patience to bat for that long. I batted for 408 minutes, and struck just seven boundaries, in making 129. Berry, at the other end, was 201 not out when we eventually declared at 406 for 6.

That was in reply to Transvaal's 290 all out. The game ended in a draw, but it was memorable to me, because it opened my account of first-class hundreds.

Clearly, that marathon innings knocked some sense into me, because most of my subsequent first-class hundreds after that involved a lot more boundaries, and a lot less time at the wicket! But, as a youngster in his first season of grown-up cricket, I loved every minute. Transvaal had a strong bowling attack, and the boys back in the hut greeted us with great gusto when we came back in at the end of day two.

Transvaal always had several international players in their line-up and were formidable, so the fact that we had resisted being blown away meant a lot to the side. We ended up sharing the Currie Cup that season with Transvaal, so though we only drew that return leg at Kingsmead, the fact that we didn't lose the match made all the difference.

I was loving every second of the grown-up cricket. Barry and I were going through many fundamental stages of our careers together, but perhaps a reminder of our youthful nature then was the fact that we were both having a terrible time running between the wickets.

There was never a problem of us running each other out, but we did seem to have issues judging singles when we were batting with someone else, especially in that debut season. I guess we could just put it down to youthful exuberance!

By the end of that 1965/66 season, I was very sure that I wanted to be a professional cricketer. The Rovers set-up at the time was formidable. We had Roy McLean as captain, as well as Peter Carlstein and Lee Irvine, just to name a few. I had joined Rovers straight after school, and it was up there with first-class cricket for intensity.

Most of our games were at Kingsmead, because the ground wasn't used much for marquee matches. In those days, there was another field next to the world-class stadium that Kingsmead is now. The South Stand wasn't there, obviously, and where the SABC studios of today are situated, there was a second ground, where another club match would take place at the same time. So, even though you couldn't quite see what was going on, you could hear from the cheers and the appeals how your rivals were getting on.

The Kingsmead that we played on in those days had a reputation for being just as fast as the Wanderers, and I thoroughly enjoyed bowling there. At Hilton, I had started bowling with a bit of gas, but I soon realised after school that I needed to get through a few more gears to trouble the really good players. I would bowl faster and faster depending on the length of my run-up, and so the legend of me kicking off the sightscreen to bowl was born.

I've seen some of the run-ups in modern cricket being quite long. Shoaib Akhtar of Pakistan, for example, seemed to run in forever, but I can understand the logic behind it. To me, it was like an aeroplane charging down the runway. You needed to get as much momentum going towards the crease, so when you let that ball go, it was at full tilt!

It is hard to say whether I loved bowling or batting more. Certainly, before the knees started to take a heavy toll, I loved to do each equally as much. Later in my career I started bowling some effective off-spin once I had bowled a spell at full steam with the new ball.

Over the years, a lot of people have asked me how I became an all-rounder. It is an easy enough answer; I simply loved every aspect of the game, and tried to be as involved as I could, be it with bat or ball. I lived for the confrontation between bat and ball from an early age, and I didn't even need an opponent to get the conflict going!

I don't have a practical explanation to explain my action, as they say, but my brother Anton is adamant there is a theory behind it. Many people assumed I bowled off the wrong foot, which I never actually did. Because of my very quick arm action, and not using much body, it appeared as if I was maybe bowling off the wrong foot, but it never really phased me, either way. To be fair, he probably observed the formative stages of my action a lot closer than anyone else, as is the case with siblings. He was a first-class cricketer himself, which was no real surprise to me, because we grew up holding the feistiest of background battles in our yard. Cricket, rugby, football, golf; we played as many sports as we could when we were growing up. Each held their own fascination, their own set of rules to understand and respect, but nothing held a torch to cricket.

For us as brothers, it was pretty simple. You would bat for as long as possible and then, when you did eventually get out, you tried to get your brother out again swiftly, so you could go back to piling up the runs. It probably explains my approach to batting during my professional career. I loved batting under pressure, when it was backs to the wall, and that was probably because I had spent an entire childhood getting ready for the strain of batting for your existence. Despite the limitless number of matches that we played against each other, I also quite enjoyed having matches against myself. I, like many other youngsters around the world, had read Sir Don Bradman's book, about how he had worked on his batting as a kid by throwing a golf ball against a corrugated iron structure, and the unpredictability made his eye very sharp.

I didn't have quite the same corrugated iron to work with, but the back wall had variable bounce off the bricks, and I made it that much more interesting by bowling the ball, and then quickly picking up the bat to play a shot off the ricochet. For many a summer, I would hold private Test matches in the garden, playing off the face-brick wall with a tennis ball and a bat. Anton would laugh, but these were deadly serious affairs. Sometimes, it would be the Springboks against Australia, at Kingsmead. On other occasions, the Springboks would be in England, playing at Lord's. It wasn't enough for me that I was playing at the finest grounds in the world in my head, I also needed both teams at full strength – and I had to mimic each action, and bat left- or right-handed, depending on the batsman at the crease. It may have looked complicated from the outside, but it made perfect sense in my head, and every match was a thriller.

It was there, during those matches, that Anton reckons I started the habit of bowling off the wrong foot. Because I had to very quickly release the ball, then pick up the bat to play the shot as the ball shot back at me, I was already taking a step towards the bat as I let the ball go. So, I would supposedly bowl 'off the wrong foot', so I could be in time to play the shot, and that habit stuck with me forever. I can't dispute it, because it does make sense. But it also illustrated to me how obsessed I was with the game, even at that early stage. I had no idea how far I would eventually go but, like millions of kids have done over the decades, I was playing out the greatest battles I could conjure up in my head every day.

Of course, at that young age, I also hadn't made a firm decision as to being a spinner or a speedster. In fact, in my first year at high school, I played as a wicketkeeper/batsman! I eventually opened the bowling for Hilton, mainly because there weren't too many options. I had started trying to bowl as fast as I could when I was still playing my private Test matches in the back garden, but I had never given it much thought in terms of specialising. The spin option did stay with me, though, and there were times where I would take the new ball, and then bowl a bit of off-spin later, if the wicket was taking some turn.

That meant that I had to quickly understand the need to get fit, and stay fit for the strains and pains that came with being a fast bowler. It looks like a lot of fun when you see someone gliding in, and the action is smooth, and the ball flies past the ear, but there is a lot of pain to endure. People often say that you must look at a lock forward's ears to see how tough a game rugby is. I'd say that the heels and toes of a fast bowler pretty much fall into the same category. They tell a story of patience, perseverance and pain, all for the good of the team. The best way to try and prevent that is by getting your body strong, and then maintaining that fitness.

These days, star bowlers have physios, training programmes and eating plans. For us, it was pretty simple, especially when we got to county cricket. In those early days, the captain would give me licence to just charge in and bowl as fast as I could. My front-on action was perfect for late in-swing, and whenever I played against someone for the first time, I would invariably look to surprise them with the very late in-ducker.

I remember playing against Bill Lawry, in a crucial Test at the Wanderers, in 1966/67. Lawry was left-handed, and was respected as a very good 'leaver' of the ball. I naturally took it away from him, so the idea was to try and nick him off to the slips or gully.

On that day, bowling over the wicket, he had left the ball very well, and it was very difficult to hit the wickets. If I started the ball outside leg stump to try and get the right angle, then the ball wouldn't swing at all. As swing bowlers around the world will know, no matter how much you can bend it, there comes a point where you take the ball too far, and it just doesn't swing.

When I switched to around the wicket, I found immediate joy against Lawry, with the very first ball. I had decided not to even try and swing it, and held it across the seam, focussing purely on the right line and length. Bill went to play it, then must have figured I was taking it away from him again. He shouldered arms at the last second and, of course, the ball kept on its line. It was the perfect bluff, and it hit the top of off stump.

For me, it was very satisfying, because it was the perfect delivery in the circumstances. If it had been a touch shorter or fuller, he probably would have played it, because he would have seen the way the ball was tracking. It just happened to be the perfect line and length. That kind of dismissal, at the highest level, was purely down to the years of graft that we had to put in at club and first-class level.

I really loved my time at Natal, because we had some hard blokes who played the game in the right manner. I learnt a heck of a lot just from sitting in the changing room after a day's play and listening to the stories of old. Jackie McGlew was a terrific leader, and one who encouraged both Barry and I to be the best we could be. He always said I should bowl as hard and as fast as I could. With that advice from a national captain, I wasn't about to hold anything back!

Though we shared the Currie Cup in 1965/66, we made sure of taking the trophy for ourselves the next season, and the season after that, too! Playing cricket all year round was helping to accelerate my influence on games, with bat and ball. That 1966/67 season saw me called up for the South African Test side to take on Simpson's touring party, which led to that shouldered arms dismissal of Bill Lawry.

I have terrific memories of the Currie Cup and Natal, but in 1969/70, I made the decision to move to Cape Town, to play for Western Province. Barry and I were still the only real 'professional cricketers' of the time, because everyone else had day jobs.

Stellenbosch University had approached me with an offer to play for them, which obviously meant the chance to play for Western Province. It was a change of scenery, and a fresh challenge for me to make a mark elsewhere, and coaching was something that I hadn't really got into at that stage.

That season at Newlands was another great experience, playing alongside one of the real bulldogs of South African cricket, the late, great Eddie Barlow.

Bunter, as he was affectionately known, was a great character on the field. He cajoled the troops from behind the stumps, and had a terrific sense of humour. Bunter was also not shy of telling the bowlers when they were slacking off, and he often inspired a wicket with a well-timed choice of phrase to get us fired up.

Bunter was just as formidable off the park, and many a Cape evening were soaked in with a few cold ones in his company. Even back then, before the ground was upgraded, Newlands had a natural beauty and charm that you couldn't beat. It was probably the best batting ground in the country, and if you got in on a hot day, the fielding side were in for a long haul!

That season was very special, and we ended up sharing the Currie Cup with Transvaal. During the course of the season, we had a hilarious incident when we played against Eastern Province. Andre Bruyns, who I played with at Stellenbosch, had become a good friend. Andre was a bit concerned about facing Peter Pollock, who had a formidable bouncer. EP also had Sibley McAdam in their ranks, who was also quite sharp and bouncy.

So, Andre asked me to go to the nets and throw down a few short balls at him, to get him ready. You must remember that these were the days before helmets, so a batman had to keep his eye on the ball and use his reflexes to not get hurt. I was throwing from about 15 metres away, and he had ducked a few confidently enough, when he suddenly decided to try and hook one.

I sconed him on the head, and he went down like a sack of potatoes! Luckily, it happened at practice, a few days before the match and he wasn't too badly hurt. He was fine to play in the match, but unfortunately, he didn't make too many runs. But he also didn't get out to Peter!

I made amends for felling our number three batsman in the nets by making 124 out of a total of 327, batting at number five. It was my first hundred at Newlands, and I understood why so many said it was a great batting ground.

I was to later make 155 for Western Province against the touring Australians at the end of that season, and that was another most enjoyable knock. I came to the crease at 68 for 3 after the Aussies had declared on 354. Mike Bowditch and I put on over 100 for the fourth wicket to get back into the match.

Once I had reached three figures, I went on the attack, smashing Ashley Mallett for five sixes in a row. The softly-spoken off-spinner was ironically nicknamed 'Rowdy', because he never really said much, but he couldn't have been too pleased when I went on the charge.

Barry Richards told me a hilarious chirp from Doug Walters which occurred in that match. Barry went to play in Australia, of course, and they relayed the story to him, which he then shared with me in later years. The Aussies were always razor-sharp on the field, even to each other. After I had hit Mallett for five sixes to end his over, Walters apparently ran past him and gave him a grave warning.

'I think you're in a spot of bother, Rowdy! It looks like he's finished with the reds, and he's moving on to the colours,' he smirked, using some snooker parlance!

We ended up drawing that match, and it marked the end of a most enjoyable season for me in the Cape. I had been part of the South African team that had trounced the Aussies 4-0, we had shared the Currie Cup with Transvaal in my first season at Western Province, and I had finally got the chance to spend some time at the wicket later in the season. I batted down the order for the national team, so didn't get too many chances, so when I got back to Western Province, I was pleased to notch two hundreds – one against Eastern Province, and the other against the touring Aussies.

Living in Cape Town had also been a pleasurable experience, as we had been put up in a rondavel house, in the middle of a wine farm in Stellenbosch, which is a magnificent part of the world. In the summer, with the long days and cool evenings, there was no better place to be.

By the next season, a new challenge had presented itself, and we were off once more, to set up camp in Rhodesia, where there were some wonderful memories made.

Chapter 10

Rhodesia and a return to my roots

URING THE 1970 English season, a very interesting challenge was put in front of me. Rhodesia (as they were known back then) were in the B division of the Currie Cup, but had ambitions of breaking through into the top table of South African cricket, and they offered me a contract to be part of their plans.

I wasn't really sure why there had to be two divisions, because with four or five teams in each division, we could have had one really strong division. As it was, my time in Rhodesia was full of great friends and, as fate would have it, some of my greatest performances with bat and ball.

We actually won the Currie Cup, in 1971/72, but it was later taken away from us by the South African Cricket Union. We had won promotion to the A division the previous year, which was my first season, and were keen to build on that success. There was a particularly feisty contest against Eastern Province, who were usually led by Graeme Pollock. But, on that occasion, Graeme was out with injury, and Lorrie Wilmot was the skipper.

It was a tense affair, nonetheless, and it came down to EP setting us a target of around 324 in the last four and a half hours of play. That roughly translated to about 70 overs, and a run-rate heading towards five an over. Those kinds of numbers were unheard of in those days, but we decided to have a dip anyway.

By tea-time, we were somehow still in with a fighting chance, and Wilmot and his team realised that they were in trouble. The playing rules had changed that season, and they deemed that once the last hour was called, there were 20 overs left in the match. So, Eastern Province started to slow things down, aware that once that last hour started, the 20 overs were non-negotiable.

They had a bloke called Claude Pittaway bowling, and he took an age between overs. The final hour was due to start at 4:45pm, and he had started bowling the last over just before that time. So we figured that 20 overs would begin after his over. I was batting at the time, and I made a point of going to the umpires and confirming that the 20 overs couldn't have started with his over. The umpires agreed. At the end of his over, there was a drinks break. The two captains and the umpires had a brief discussion to confirm the 20-over scenario, just to be sure. We were right in it, and by the time there was one over left, we were six wickets down, but only needed six runs to win.

It was extraordinary. Rhodesia was about to win the Currie Cup A division, and an expectant crowd had gathered to see in the historic moment at the Queen's Club. I was on about 70 not out, and Paddy Cliff was on about 20. We touched base between overs, and then I went back to take strike.

As I looked up, I realised that the whole Eastern Province team were in the covers. Initially, I thought that was part of their strategy to starve us of runs, but then I saw them all marching off the field.

They were walking off, as if the game was over. It was astonishing! The crowd went bonkers, and they were baying for blood, and with good reason, too. Eastern Province were adamant that they had already bowled the 20 overs for the last hour and, in their minds, the umpires were wrong. I felt that it wasn't for them to make such a call. The umpires were the law, after all.

And, as far as we were concerned, a team that walked off the field before umpires had called time were forfeiting the game, which meant that we had to be awarded the match. We were left to pacify a fuming crowd, but as far as we knew, we had won the match.

At the end of the season, the whole matter was reviewed. Both teams had to submit a report to the South African Cricket Union. They, in their wisdom, decided to overrule the umpires, concluding that the match was in fact a draw. The title went to Transvaal, as a result, and one couldn't help but think that if we had been any other province, things may have panned out very differently. The whole matter left a very bitter taste at the end of an amazing season for us.

My time at Rhodesia had many more highlights, though, on and off the field. The International Wanderers had come out from the UK for a tour, and they came over to play us, too. They were led by Brian Close, of England acclaim, and there was a hilarious incident involving rugby coaching guru Ian McIntosh, who was still playing for Rhodesia at the time.

The Queen's Club in Bulawayo was heaving, just after the day's play. Closey and his mob had become quite merry, singing songs, and playing a few drinking games, which they challenged us to match. There was one guy who had managed to down a beer without using his hands, which we thought was quite impressive, considering that it was tricky enough to down one with a hand after a long day on the field.

While we stood pondering what to do to match this great sporting feat, Mac came to our rescue. A few of the cricketers were close to him, and I had met him on occasion. Mac demanded that the bar be cleared of all the glasses. The bar was at least 20 metres, and it stretched on to the terrace area, which was full of patrons that day.

We stood, as perplexed as the Wanderers, pondering what Mac had up his sleeve. I thought he might swallow dive all the way along the bar, but it was quite high for that sort of manoeuvre. What occurred next was incredible.

Mac took a long run-up, and at full speed, dived head-first, straight over the bar! There was silence, as we worried about his wellbeing, but Mac popped up, beaming from ear to ear, as if it was the most natural thing in the world. There was thunderous applause – and a fair bit of relief – from the entire gallery at his athleticism. Closey, having been rather boisterous before, was gobsmacked.

'There is no way we are going to even try to match that,' he bellowed, and he and his boys went back to regular drinking!

Things were going swimmingly on the field, too. In 1970, I had a proper purple patch with the bat, when I scored six first-class hundreds in a row. I had no idea it was some sort of record until I was told that I had matched Sir Donald Bradman and CB Fry.

The amazing run started against Natal, with a quick-fire 119 in Bulawayo. I then continued that form with 129 against Transvaal B, at Salisbury, a wicket I always enjoyed. We had to wait a month for our next game, a trek to Bloemfontein, to play Free State. We rolled them for 66, and I made my third ton in a row, with 107.

I still had no idea that it was a run that was heading towards the record books. The time between games also didn't help to keep up! New Year's Day in 1971 was pretty special, as I pummelled 174 against North Eastern Transvaal, which was my highest score up to that point, and was particularly special because the team had been in trouble at 56 for 3.

We went hunting for diamonds in Kimberley next, and a few of the boys were ribbing me, saying that I could get five in a row. I was just happy to be seeing it well, and to be also getting amongst the wickets. We were playing some of our best cricket as a team, and the De Beers Oval reaped another ton.

The sixth ton, as it turned out, was the most significant. It was a good two months after Kimberley, and again we were on the back foot. Playing against Western Province, on a lively Salisbury wicket, I came in at 5 for 3. Someone mentioned to me that only Bradman and Fry had scored six in six, but I wasn't too concerned with that just then.

We were still in trouble as a team, so I flayed on, eventually being dismissed for 254 and, more importantly, we ended up winning the match by an innings. I was knackered, but extremely chuffed to have stood up when the team really needed me to do so. Though I was never treated as an overseas player at Rhodesia, I felt that responsibility as the 'pro'.

I never played for individual records, but looked to advance the fortunes of the team whenever I had a bat or ball in my hand. Throughout that patch, I just felt in a very good place, and decided to ride the wave for as long as it carried me.

The early 70s were a conflicting time. I was at the peak of my playing powers, but South Africa was in political turmoil, and it had already dawned on me in 1970 that we may never play Test cricket again, unless the government drastically changed its policies. There were horrible things happening to the vast majority of the population, which put our own ambitions into sharp perspective. But, truth be told, the political ramifications were beyond our control as mere cricketers.

With no more international cricket on the agenda, we threw everything into the Currie Cup again. I managed to score 500 runs and take 50 wickets in successive seasons, in 1971/72, and 1972/73. I even manged to nab a record 59 scalps in that 72/73 campaign.

People have often asked how I think our potential side in the 70s would have fared against the West Indians of the 80s, but it is a difficult question to answer. I actually felt that the side we could have had in the 70s might have been even stronger than the one we had in the 1969/70 series against Australia. The emergence of Clive Rice, Vince van der Bijl, Garth le Roux and Denys Hobson – to name but a few – coupled with a few other guys in their prime, would have given us a very strong side.

We will never know, of course, but I cannot grumble, because the World Series did provide a glimpse of what could have been, if our country's shameful regime hadn't ensured that we were left in the international wilderness for all those years.

While at Rhodesia, I also fondly remember an incident involving Peter Carlstein, who had played for years with Transvaal. Peter was quite a character, but very talented on the field. He thrived on a bit of needle to get him going, as it helped his concentration.

When we played against his former side, they made sure not to speak to him. It was very obviously a tactic to wind him up, and he was met with silence as he walked to the wicket. He took guard, and braced himself to be met with some early chirp. Not a word was said to him, and he was already getting a bit fidgety.

The bowler was left-armer Willy Kerr, and just as Kerr was about to run in, skipper Ali Bacher stopped him. Ali moved the field around, and the rest of the fielders maintained their silence. Peter, getting increasingly annoyed by the lack of dialogue, took his guard again, and walked down the wicket to tap away at the turf, to make his own point.

Keeper Lee Irvine was standing up to Kerr, and was also not saying a word to the batsman, even though Peter was so close that you could hear him grunting to himself. Once Peter was ready, Willy Kerr again started running in, and Ali again stopped him from mid-off.

By now, all of us in the batting dressing room were intrigued by the melodrama. Ali changed the field again, apologised to the umpire, and Willy finally ran in. He served up a decent delivery, which Peter defended solidly towards Ali at mid-off.

As the ball trundled off, Lee Irvine couldn't help himself, and muttered something.

'Another glorious stroke-player here, boys,' he piped up.

Peter, silently raging at what had been going on, didn't need a second invitation. He promptly turned on the keeper, and thrust the full force of the bat handle into Lee's chest. The poor keeper was doubled over, and the umpires had to intervene. Peter was fuming, but the Transvaal side knew they had got to him. It was a crazy episode, but we got on with the game eventually. And, despite the madness at the start of his innings, Peter still managed to make 90 in that knock!

That same match had a lot going on, actually, as it was also the scene of my career-best figures of 9-71. I had started the habit of bowling occasional off-spin on pitches that were assisting. On this particular occasion, Transvaal had roped in a Welshman, David Lewis, who was a leg-spinner, and had enjoyed some success on the club scene, and manager Jonny Waite was clearly hoping that he could replicate that against us.

He hadn't had a great game with the ball, and hadn't managed to pick up a wicket in either innings. Apparently Lewis later complained to his wife, saying that he didn't think Ali was that good a captain, because he kept on taking him out of the attack – just as the leggie was finding his range! Lee Irvine, who was in the best seat to observe Lewis, remembers that he spent a lot of time diving on both sides of the wicket, desperate to save some byes!

Having batted first, our bowlers had a lot of rough to work with in the second innings, and that is when I decided to bowl off-spin. I removed Norman Featherstone with the new ball, caught behind, but was soon working the rough with my off-spin.

After Richie Kaschula had Ali Bacher out, I found joy from the turning track, settling on a good length. I bowled the left-handed Lee Irvine with one that went round his legs out of the rough area, but most of the other wickets were fairly normal procedure on a third-day wicket with wear and tear.

Unbeknown to us, David Lewis had already been handed a very hasty tutorial on playing off-spin, administered by manager Jonny Waite in the tennis courts, behind the changing rooms. They obviously knew that it may come down to him, and were trying to equip him as best they could.

I had always had it in my mind to run in and bowl full tilt to the tail-enders. You could take a ball or three getting your line and lengths right with spin, but bowling pace was usually the best way to a quick finish.

As he nervously walked to the crease, expecting to face some off-spin, I started pacing out my full run-up, ready to kick of the scoreboard. It must have dawned on him that the last hour of prep in the tennis courts had been a bit of a waste of time.

I was only interested in getting the final wicket and wrapping up the match, so I charged in. The ball clattered into his pads and they scurried a leg-bye. It was also the end of my over, leaving Kaschula with six balls at Lewis. He survived the over and we were starting to worry about running out of balls. I had an over, and then there was just one more from Kaschula for Transvaal to survive and draw the match. I went back to bowling off-spin, and I promptly cleaned up the final wicket of Danny Bekker, to finish with a career-best 9-71. It had been a tense end to a crazy match, one that had plenty of memories for all of us to look back on with a chuckle.

Rhodesia was certainly one of the best periods of my career, for so many reasons. And I wouldn't change a thing about it. But my first-class career didn't end there, as it took me back to where it all began for a Natal swansong.

After the World Series, I came back to Durban, playing Currie Cup cricket for Natal. Vince van der Bijl was captain by then, and he did a very good job. We didn't win the Currie Cup that season, but we did so the following year.

There was one hilarious story involving a young Adrian Kuiper, when we played against Western Province, which Vince van der Bijl reminds me of. Kuiper was a promising batsman, who we had heard could play his strokes, so I had tested his mettle in the first innings with a bouncer, which he hooked instinctively, but was caught down at long-leg. We knew that he had it on his mind as he came out the second time around.

Vince made a point of ambling over to me, at the top of my run, to discuss the field that we would set. Kuiper had already taken guard by then, and was waiting for me to come in. All batsmen know that the innings after a duck is one that you want to start as soon as possible, and Vince knew that drawing it out would not help Kuiper's nerves.

We made it very clear that the strategy would revolve around short balls again, with a long-leg, and another man on the square-leg fence. There was a short-leg, and then Vince added in a leg gully, just to emphasise the point. All of this was done very deliberately, and then Vince walked away towards mid-off.

Kuiper settled at the crease, and I came charging in. He pre-empted the bouncer, and was practically ducking as I let it go. To his great surprise, however, I bowled a looping slower ball, straight at the stumps.

Kuiper was already crouched, waiting for the ball to whizz by. It must have seemed like super slow motion to him, as he saw the ball heading straight to him, and then clip the stumps. Vince and I took great delight in the double bluff, and it again proved that mind games can be very effective in cricket.

Speaking of mind games, there was another game of mischief in the 1979/80 season, against the powerhouse Transvaal unit. They had Jimmy Cook, Graeme Pollock, Clive Rice, Kevin McKenzie, Allan Kourie and Ray Jennings in a formidable side, which later earned the nickname the 'Mean Machine'.

Between Vince and the senior players in the Natal side, we decided to prepare a turning track at Kingsmead for the match – which was unheard of back in those days, considering our seam attack, consisting of Vince, Kenny Cooper, Paddy Clift and myself.

For this match, however, we loaded our side with the left-arm spin of Baboo Ebrahim and John Muil. The groundsman was the wonderful Jay Pillay, and he did an outstanding job in preparing the turner that we had requested. Transvaal arrived the day before the game, and we asked Jay not to show them the strip until the very last minute.

On a gloriously hot day, without a cloud in the sky, the covers were still on the wicket, much to the bemusement of our visitors. They naturally wanted to have a look at it. By the time they had finished practising, Jay didn't have any other option but to take the covers off, and reveal the big secret to Transvaal.

The pitch resembled the golden sand just down the road on North Beach, surrounded by the lush green grass of the rest of the field. There was pandemonium in the Transvaal ranks, and they immediately phoned Johannesburg, urgently requesting another spinner to be sent down. The only other slow bowler in their side was Allan Kourie.

Kevin Kerr was the man chosen to answer the SOS from Durban. Unfortunately for us, the visitors won the toss, and elected to bat first. Although we had them 30-odd for 3, they ended up scoring over 350, with Graeme Pollock notching 168 and Clive Rice 110.

The rest, as they say is history! We were bowled out for 150 by Kerr and Kourie in the first innings, and managed to do a little bit better in the second innings, at least making Transvaal bat again. We still lost by ten wickets, as we were undone by their spin twins!

It wasn't very funny at the time, but we eventually laughed at ourselves in due course. Our strengths lay in pace bowling, and gambling on the toss of a coin had come back to bite us – hard! The whole episode was all rather embarrassing.

By the next season, we won the Currie Cup by relying on our traditional strengths, which were to play on a normal, green wicket in Durban. In those days, Currie Cup matches lasted three days with a seven-hour day. It was also standardised around the country, starting at 10am everywhere, and ending at 6pm.

As everyone knows, with the weather in Durban, the chances of starting at 10am and not losing any time in the match was very unlikely. So, as senior players, we reckoned it was necessary to prepare wickets that hurried the game along. That meant some very green wickets, which led to the emergence of the 'Green Mamba' phenomenon.

To give you an idea of the state of the Kingsmead wicket, Vince van der Bijl took 54 wickets at 9.5 and Kenny Cooper 38 wickets at 13 apiece. Those kinds of numbers don't come about on flat wickets, that's for sure! And, at the other end of the scale, Chris Wilkins scored the most runs during that season, with 595 at an average of 54. Chris got his runs by being attacking whenever he got the chance.

When we played at Kingsmead, we had come to accept that preparing green tops meant that the ball would do a bit more. Our batsmen understood that the bat would be beaten from time to time, but that they shouldn't let it bother them too much. When the chance to play strokes was there, we wouldn't hold back.

Visitors to Kingsmead went the other way, retreating into their shells, and trying to ride out the storm. We had learnt our lesson with the dry wicket comedy, and we were now using the conditions to the very best of our ability.

A prime example of this was the game against Eastern Province, who put us in to bat on the 'Mamba', and we made 250. In response, they were rolled over for 69 and 101. Their defensive batting approach played into our hands perfectly.

My time in Durban also had me playing club cricket for Glenwood Old Boys. We had a great time, and there was a great sense of camaraderie around the club. There was one particularly good night we had, having won the league.

Tradition dictated that, after the fines meeting, we went back to the bar with the regular patrons. At some point in the evening, each player was then required to down a beer in celebration. Things were getting a bit out of hand, and it was getting late, and I snuck out without saying goodbye.

I went to get in to my car, but couldn't find it. I sheepishly came back into the bar, told the guys that my car was missing, and they asked me to take them to where I had parked it. When we went back to the spot, there it was, parked exactly where I had left it that morning. It had clearly been one heck of a night!

Another significant highlight in my second stint for Natal was the hundred I made in 1983 against the West Indian rebel side. Coming in at 67 for 4, against an attack that included three fast-bowling Test caps in Ezra Moseley, Colin Croft and Bernard Julien, I made 102, out of a total of 230, and I immediately felt comfortable at the crease. Given that it was played on our typical 'Green Mamba', it was full of strokes, especially against that attack!

It turned out to be my final first-class century, giving me a pair of Natal centuries as the book-ends to all my tons around the world. Come to think of it, my last was in complete contrast to the maiden hundred, which had been a slow, dogged affair in my first season of Currie Cup cricket.

I took just as much pride in the last as I did in my first, and I felt it was fitting that both were in Natal colours.

Chapter 11

The World Series revolution

T HE GAME we all hold so dearly is always changing. A lot of advancements have happened in the last decade or so, but I still look back fondly on being part of the biggest mindshift the game had ever seen, in the form of World Series, in the late 70s. Coming towards the end of my career, it was a terrific barometer for me personally, but also a wonderful advertisement of where the game could go with a bit more imagination.

World Series Cricket will forever hold a special place in my heart because, without a doubt, it was the toughest level of cricket I ever played. As South Africans of that time, Test cricket wasn't really an option but, even if it had been, World Series was another step up. It was the brainchild of Kerry Packer, of course, and though it may not have been granted first-class status initially, it changed the game as we knew it forever. I was relieved to see the change of heart by the ICC, when they recognised the matches played under the World Series banner.

In my mind, if those matches between Australia and the Rest of the World XI could be granted Test status, then World Series deserved to be granted the same level of importance, even belatedly. No one who was a part of it ever saw it as a hit and giggle, or a money-making scheme for players who were past their best. It was tough, uncompromising stuff, but with bells and whistles that made it an intriguing offer to us as players. When you see the fanfare around the IPL now, you realise just how big a marketing tool cricket is. The game is always searching for new ways to keep people hooked nowadays; T20 cricket, day-night Test matches, players hooked up to the commentary to give viewers an insight. Back then, in the late 70s, Packer was revolutionary, and the impact that his World Series Cricket made was significant.

The first time I met him was at the Savoy Hotel in London, which was already a far cry from the pub lunch fare that cricketers were accustomed to in those days. I went with the late Tony Greig, then England captain, who Packer had shrewdly scouted as his main recruiting agent.

The late Eddie Barlow, or Bunter as we knew him, came along to the meeting, too. There was a fair amount of intrigue amongst us, because this whole process was still under wraps. But we knew that there was something up. Greigy was clearly excited by something, and we were keen to find out just what had brought a couple of county cricketers to one of London's finest hotels.

'Greigy' was quite a character. His involvement with Packer was met with huge criticism in England, but he immediately saw an opportunity to try something completely different. As an England captain, crossing the line to support an Australian initiative was ballsy, to say the least, but the Tony Greig that I knew always backed himself.

Back at the Savoy, that Sunday afternoon, I was immediately impressed by what was on the table, and even more excited at the potential of playing at a level that South Africans couldn't hope for, and soon signed on. Though it may seem like peanuts in today's world of million-dollar players, the (Aus) $25,000 fee for each player was life-changing back then. What's more, Packer dangled the carrot of a winning bonus, which ensured that every game had an edge, when we eventually got to playing.

To this day, the fact that Packer and his team managed to maintain the huge veil of secrecy around the whole thing amazes me. In the modern world of Twitter and the countless other forms of social media, it would have been impossible. You can just imagine trying to get every porter at a hotel in London to stay silent about spotting some of the biggest names in the game today sitting around a table with a successful and ambitious businessman.

But, somehow, Packer and about 60–70 people who knew somehow managed to keep a lid on this huge coup for months, even with some of the biggest names in the game involved. Packer's sincerity was proved when he backed Greigy, John Snow and I in a challenge we took to the High Court against the England authorities, who were threatening to ban us from first-class cricket if we took part in 'Packer's Circus'.

Greigy must also be given a lot of credit for the stance he took. He was a massive figure in the game, and the sudden emergence of this 'circus' was obviously a huge threat to the establishment. It forced them to look at players in a different way, as entertainers instead of just staff, and they didn't take kindly to being forced into it by an Australian magnate.

Those were difficult times, for all of us, but especially for the English players. It meant putting their Test credentials, and their credibility at risk. For us, as South Africans, the World Series window fitted conveniently with our playing commitments, and I remember us having a quiet chuckle that it was one of the few times that it came in handy to be a South African cricketer during that era.

During those tense times in and out of court, Packer struck me as a man who was as good as his word. Once the legal ramifications had been dealt with, he asked me to name the South Africans I thought could add value to the competition, and then made one phone call to get them on a plane, and their money sorted.

Graeme Pollock and Denys Hobson were selected, but they never got to play, because the West Indian contingent were uncomfortable because they played their cricket exclusively in South Africa. Of course, Graeme and Dennis were never interested in politics. They had only ever wanted to play cricket. It was an unfortunate stand-off, but the West Indians, with a full team of stars, held sway.

It was a great pity, because it robbed a wider audience of the chance of seeing Graeme Pollock showcase his talents on a bigger stage. He was easily one of the best batsmen I ever saw, and certainly the most elegant. That giant front stride simply anchored down the wicket, and his exquisite timing caressed the ball through the covers. It was a pity the appreciative crowds of Australia never got the chance to see more of him in later years, though they had seen him when he toured with South Africa in 1963/64.

As it was, Packer still saw to it that Graeme and Dennis got their money, but our team would have been even more formidable with them in tow. The biggest attraction for us as players was, obviously, the financial reward. When we, as the Rest of the World XI, won the 'SuperTest' final against Australia at the SCG in 1979, we felt like we had won the lottery, as we were going to share (Aus) $100,000 on top of our series fee.

In many ways, you could say the World Series was the original IPL. For those players nearing the end of distinguished careers, World Series Cricket afforded one last hurrah. Coloured clothing, white balls, playing under lights… Packer had his detractors, but you couldn't knock him for being innovative.

That visual impact, as well as the attention and revenue that it created, immediately changed the face of cricket, as it forced the administrators of the game to change their outlook at players, and the rewards they got from the game they served so well. It wasn't just the players that Packer's World Series changed things for, though.

Nowadays, players' wives, girlfriends and even family are part and parcel of extended tours or major tournaments. They travel with the players, get prime tickets to games, and form a strong part of the touring party when they are there. Packer started that with us, and it was a touch that went down a treat with all of us. To have our families around, as we went off on this new adventure, certainly brought the best out of us.

For me personally, it was a great thrill to have Maryna and the kids waiting at the hotel after a long day, and the kids certainly struck up some great friendships during those hours in the stands with other youngsters watching their daddies.

Some may beg to differ but, to my mind, World Series was a far tougher examination of one's skills than the IPL, simply because of the sheer weight of quality on offer. In the IPL, you may have two or three genuine world stars on each team, but during the World Series, everywhere you looked, there was a genuine star. Of course, the IPL is a different format altogether, and the intensity in the middle is always there, regardless of the level of cricket.

Somewhere there will be a club match happening in the world where teams are ready to tear into each other, such is the competitive nature of this great game of ours. In my entire playing career, though, the World Series was the stage where that intensity was felt more than ever. There was just no respite.

To make matters even more demanding, the hours that we had to play made for very long days. For the SuperTests, we had day-night affairs, which would start at 1:00pm and finish at 10:30pm. On grounds like VFL Park, which was outside Melbourne's city hub, it meant a drive of an hour just to get there before play. When you hear the concerns for the modern pink ball under lights, in this new format of day-night cricket, I can't help but look back on our days facing West Indian giants, who towered over sight-screens, bowling with a murky ball in the twilight.

It was the school of hard knocks, but that was the brief. That was when the crowd was coming in from a day at work, and expected to see a couple of hours of rich entertainment, just like they are looking to capitalise on with these Test matches in Adelaide and other cities around the world.

The actual playing time was seven and a half hours for the four-day SuperTests, and it was all designed to fit into the prime-time TV slot that Packer wanted to dominate. The playing hours also amounted to 30 hours over four days, which was the same length of playing time as a five-day Test match. By the time play was done, and we had taken the bus back to the hotel, it was almost midnight by the time you got back to the hotel, especially at places like VFL Park, which was an hour outside Melbourne. After playing in that sort of intensity, it then takes you a couple of hours at least before you are ready for bed. And, at the back of your mind, you knew that you had to get up and do it all again the next day. So there definitely was some grief to go with the supposed glamour.

Some people had the misconception that the World Series was just a glorified hit and giggle. It was anything but; there were the long playing hours, for one thing, and we certainly earned our crust off the field too. There were commercial engagements, corporate functions and other things that we had to partake in. In that sense, Greigy did better than most, because he became a household name with his personal endorsement deals, including a breakfast cereal advertising campaign. I can just imagine the look on the Aussie team's faces waking up, and seeing Greigy smiling back at them from their box of cereal.

But that was where the smiling would end, because there was some serious speed spread amongst the three sides. At a time when helmets were still an afterthought, just looking at the attacks is still quite scary. The Aussies had Jeff Thomson, Dennis Lillee, Wayne Prior and Lenny Pascoe, who were not as well known as the former pair, but as quick as anyone else in the world at the time. Prior actually hit Barry Richards on the head later, in a rebel tour match. Barry was renowned for always having time to play his shots, so that is an indication of just how slippery Prior was as a bowler.

The West Indians were, of course, world-feared for their pace attack, and the likes of Andy Roberts, Joel 'Big Bird' Garner, Wayne Daniel and Michael 'Whispering Death' Holding gave many a batsman sleepless nights. Between the 'Bird' and 'Whispering Death' himself, you got precious little in your half as a batsman, and there was no relenting in pace. The fact that we played on the world's first drop-in pitches, under lights, with white balls that always seemed to have a more pronounced seam, made life even tougher for batsmen. The averages from the 'SuperTests' that we played between the three sides (Australia, West Indies and the Rest of the World) make for interesting reading, because some proud Test records were put under intense scrutiny.

Though we were not playing under the auspices of any formal laws, it was understood that we were operating under the first-class conditions that we were familiar with. The modern laws of the game have very strict limits on short-pitched bowling for example, but we had no discussion on limitations for short balls back then.

Captains and the crowd seemed to be almost baying for blood at times, which made for some interesting contests. One crazy encounter in the second season encapsulated the severity of the competition. The Rest of the World were taking on the West Indians at VFL Park, in Melbourne. With it not being a regular cricket ground, a drop-in pitch was used. But the groundsman had left a tinge of grass on it, and it was alarmingly lively. We only managed to score 102 all out, in just over 40 overs. Andy Roberts and Joel Garner were just about unplayable, and the Melbourne audience took great delight in seeing our batsmen struggling to cope with the heat in the middle.

This was despite Majid Khan having been taken to hospital with a broken cheekbone, having been struck by Andy Roberts. Sat in the changing room, we were further annoyed by the Channel Nine commentary at the time, which was also having a go at our supposed lack of substance. So, when we walked out to defend the total, we decided to give as good as we got.

In Garth le Roux, Imran Khan and Clive Rice, we had a pretty rapid attack of our own, and the Windies were soon hopping about, too. By the time the 'Big Bird' sauntered to the crease, the game was done, with the Windies already 67 for 9.

Like most number 11s, 'Big Bird' quite enjoyed his batting, and loved nothing more than to have a quick cameo to get the blood going before he got a bright red cherry in his hands. But he was nursing a broken finger on his left hand that day, and had told me as much in the lift on the way to the game. I had asked him if the finger had properly healed, and he said it was okay. I then chirped something to the effect that it was funny how one's niggles always found a way of getting in harm's way, just when they were about to heal. I didn't realise how prophetic it would turn out to be.

With the game just about done, we didn't expect Bird to hang around for long. Clive Rice, bowling really fast then, had four balls to go, and the instruction to him was to bowl four of the fastest bouncers he could muster. Even at nine down, there was no relenting. We had taken a hammering when we were batting, and I guess we wanted to make a statement of our own. Garner himself had made all of us look ordinary, with figures of 2-12 in ten very awkward overs. As Joel walked to the crease, Greigy confirmed with the umpire just how many balls were left. The umpire confirmed the four, and Greigy instructed Clive to deliver the four fastest bouncers he could muster.

As it was, Ricey didn't even need the four balls, as he got his first one spot on; a perfect bouncer rearing up towards Garner's face, who instinctively stuck out his bat, with the left hand absorbing the blow. Of course, the broken finger had to take most of the impact. Big Bird, fuming and in agony, turned around, and smashed out two stumps with his bat, then kicked the remaining one over, before marching off the field. And that, as they say, was that, game over, and one very angry Bird brooding in the opposition dressing room.

Our other memorable contest against the West Indies, as the Rest of the World, was when we trounced them by an innings at the Sydney Cricket Ground, in the lead-up to the 1978/79 four-day final. By all accounts, it was a full-blooded Windies Test line-up, including Viv Richards, Clive Lloyd, Andy Roberts, Joel Garner and Desmond Haynes.

What was interesting was the meeting we had as a squad before the match, which Tony Greig was a part of, as one of the leadership core. Greigy had riled the Windies as England captain, when he infamously said he would make them 'grovel'.

It was a terrible choice of words, given the history and the undertone, and the Windies were certainly justified to feel aggrieved at that phrasing. It obviously helped with their motivation for their England tour of 1976. When we met as a team, ahead of playing against an equally formidable West Indian side, we spoke about the need to try and put pressure on the Windies – a lot easier said than done, of course.

It was a far harder task to put them under sustained pressure, because they were the best team in the world, with a clutch of world-beaters. We had to try and get on top, and then stay on top for as long as possible. In that encounter in Sydney, we did just that. We piled on 471, keeping them on the field for over 160 overs. They lost Holding to injury early, which didn't help their workload. That meant Big Bird had to bowl 50 overs himself.

By the time they came to bat, they were wilting, and we dismissed them twice for not much more than 200 in each innings, having enforced the follow-on. It was fair to say that the pressure had told, and we executed the game plan that we had discussed to the last detail. The plan worked a treat on that occasion, but it did help that we won the toss on a good batting pitch, and exerted scoreboard pressure.

That is the thing with pressure. It gets to everyone, inevitably. Of course, it was a one-off game, and the West Indies were up against it for a long time. What would have been interesting is playing that formidable side in a series, and seeing how that would have panned out. They were the best in the world, without doubt, and I am sure they would have got their own back in a four- or five-match series.

World Series Cricket was relentless in that regard but, despite the ferocious nature of the action in the middle, the outstanding feature of the World Series era was the camaraderie between all the players. We had some great nights when the schedule allowed, and we certainly all enjoyed having a drink together, the ferocity of the cricket put aside for a while.

I can still recall the Christmas party of 1978, which ended up with several players dancing on tables. I remember Tony Greig, wearing long-johns and no top, with his very pale skin, arm in arm with West Indian all-rounder Collis King, built like Tarzan, who was only wearing what you could probably describe in modern terms as hot-pants. The pair of them, oblivious to the rest of the world, dancing on a table, captured exactly what the World Series was all about. Play hard on and off the field. Those were the days.

Whenever we got on the park against the Aussies, they always wanted Greigy's wicket more than anyone else's, and you could actually feel the intensity lifting whenever he walked to the crease. An incident in the second season of World Series, in 1978/79 – when we beat Australia in three days in the final – stands out as a reminder of just how much the Aussies relished the prospect of getting one over the English captain.

Our selection committee for the Rest of the World XI comprised of Tony Greig, Asif Iqbal and myself, on account of international experience and county leadership. Greigy had been left out of the previous two SuperTests, against the West Indies and Australia, due to a lack of form. He had agreed with the decision, too.

Things changed by the time we got to the final, though, as England were due to tour Pakistan during that period. Pakistan wanted to include two players from the World Series, in Majid Khan and Javed Miandad, who flew to Pakistan but ended up not being allowed to play, due to their status as Packer players. In their absence, Greigy and Eddie Barlow were selected to play in the final.

That final match had its fair dose of drama, long before the tense finish. Lillee and Pascoe were the final pair for the Aussies' second innings, and every single run they were eking out was vital, given the deteriorating nature of the wicket. Pascoe was facing Garth le Roux, and Lillee was playing cheerleader at the non-striker's end.

After every ball, Lillee would go halfway down the pitch to encourage his fellow fast bowler. On the second-to-last ball of le Roux's over, Pascoe managed to keep out a full delivery, and it dribbled to mid-off, where Derek Underwood was fielding.

'Deadly' had noticed that Lillee hadn't gone back to make his ground, and had just ventured down the wicket to have his mini conference with his partner. Derek walked up to the wickets, and told Lillee that he could actually run him out, because the ball was not dead just yet.

The Aussie fast bowler went nuts, telling Underwood where he could get off. Underwood had no intention of running him out, of course, but he was also well within his rights to give Lillee a warning. With tensions just about boiling over, Garth's next ball of that over was a slower one, and it flummoxed Pascoe, to wrap up the innings.

But, Lillee was still bristling, and he was still remonstrating with Underwood. Clive Rice and I immediately ran towards our team-mate, to help him out. Lillee turned and had a full go at us, too, waving his bat and threatening to knock our heads off shortly, supposedly when he got the ball in his hands. It never got physical, but there were some pretty heated words exchanged, and it set the tone for a tense final innings.

It was unknown to us at that time, but we were actually playing our last ever match of the revolutionary World Series. There were deals on the table for the next season, but it was only months later that we were informed that we wouldn't be playing again. It was just as well, then, that the final was as memorable an affair for us as it was.

Having been in early trouble, chasing 224 to win the final and the bonus, Barry Richards and I put on a decent partnership of just under 100 for the fourth wicket to make the game safe, having been 80 for 4 when we joined forces. We had managed to quell a charging Lillee and Pascoe, too. There were few more compelling sights than Barry in full flow with the bat, but he had largely underperformed to that point. The Aussie public, who know a good batsman when they see one, were well aware of his incredible abilities; his sensational near-hundred in one Test match session in Durban still in folklore, and then his stack of runs scored in Shield cricket had made him a legend, especially when he made 300 in a single day's play at the Waca.

With a fair bit on the line, Barry showed another side to his game, grafting his way to a dogged hundred on a pitch that was playing up and down. He wasn't fluent because the conditions didn't allow, but he saw us home. I chipped in with 44 at the other end. When I departed, I could sense that the Aussies were a bit too fired up, especially considering we only had about 40 runs to get, with five wickets in hand.

Then I clicked why there was a sudden fire in their belly; Greigy was due in next and, to make matters worse, he was on a pair. He hadn't played much in the lead-up to the final, but that hadn't stopped him from saying how good he felt ahead of the match. Our combative skipper had even gone as far as saying he was likely to make a hundred, given the form that he was in. Greigy was a lot of things, but he was never, ever short of confidence.

He had a long-running feud with his Australian counterpart Ian Chappell and, in the first innings, Greigy had only managed to face eight balls. The first seven were all sharp bouncers, and the eighth was yet another one, which he gloved in front of his face, to the keeper. It was clear that the Aussies were keen to knock him out, or get him out, whichever came first. But, to their disappointment, it was my friend Imran Khan who strolled in before the skipper.

As we closed in on the target, everyone expected us to hit the winning runs off one of Australia's quick men. To our great surprise, Chappell, with his part-time leg-spin, took the ball and proceeded to bowl the biggest wide you've ever seen, and promptly walked off the field. It was a bizarre end to what had been a particularly feisty encounter, but it was also a matter of how much the Aussies hated to lose and, perhaps, how annoyed Chappell was that it had occurred to a team led by his great adversary, Tony Greig.

There was no love lost between the two, but it was a measure of their respective standing in the game that Packer found a way to hire them both on the legendary Channel Nine commentary team. That stroke of genius paved the way for careers beyond the game for so many players, including my good friend Mark Nicholas, another Englishman who made the trek to Australia and thrived.

Greigy, often the dissenting voice amongst the Aussie choir in commentary, always made sure his point was heard, loud and clear. He revelled in the banter so much that he relocated to Australia, and was a respected authority on the game. Behind the scenes, he was a board member for Epilepsy Action Australia, having suffered from the disease from a young age. We had no idea until much later on, but his first attack was in South Africa, when he was just 14.

Men like Greig, with their influence and social standing, have done much to shed light on medical conditions that are otherwise given short shrift. In a similar vein, I have always admired the great work that golfer Ernie Els does for autism, through raising funds and awareness about the condition. Greigy's death, after a battle with lung cancer in 2012, was a great loss to the game, and he is fondly missed.

Those days of World Series Cricket were particularly important to us South Africans because that really was our ultimate stage. It gave us a shot against the best in the world at the time, and I like to think that all of our boys came out of the series with reputations enhanced.

Certainly, the fiery Garth le Roux made a mark. Having missed the first year, he promptly helped himself to man of the match in the final of 1979, and overall man of the series that season. And he was fast; as quick as anything that any side threw at us. Those who knew him in the days of domestic first-class cricket can attest that Garth was every bit as competitive as Dennis Lillee.

That said, Clive Rice was probably the most competitive player in any of the sides. There was no such thing as a lost cause in his mind, and he epitomised the hunger that so many others felt back home for big-time cricket. Given his chance at World Series level, he thrived amongst the best in the world.

Barry was, well, Barry. When he turned up in the mood, no one could bowl at him, and his hundred in that final against the Aussies was yet another reminder of his unique talents as a player. Bunter Barlow was as dependable a team man as they came, and despite being largely in charge of the touring country side, he was a crucial member of the squad as a whole. His sharp wit certainly kept everyone on their toes, and kept spirits up after tough days in the middle.

From a personal perspective, the World Series came towards the end of my fast bowling career, after over ten years on the county circuit had taken their toll. I couldn't match the others in terms of sustained pace, and I often mixed it up with some off-spin. As it was, the spin ended up getting me more wickets than the pace!

One aspect that I was really pleased about was the fact that I was able to make telling contributions with the bat during the World Series. I hadn't been afforded the chance to bat much in my fleeting Test career for South Africa, so it was nice to make decent runs against the quality of attacks that we were up against.

The success of our South African contingent was most pleasing, and gave even more reason to quietly lament what could have been if politics hadn't stopped that generation from fielding a Test side.

After that final, I had a late drink with Ricey, as well as Ian Chappell and Dennis Lillee, in the depths of the Sydney Cricket Ground changing rooms. When one considers that we were sharing drinks just hours after the heated on-field episode earlier that day, it just summed up the spirit in which the World Series was played. It was all left on the field and forgotten about, and we never held any ill-feeling or grudges against other players.

Ricey fondly relates a story from that night, but I don't remember the exact details. Ricey maintains that on that particular night, I turned to the Aussie pair and chirped, 'It's just as well that no more South Africans were playing today.'

'Why's that, mate?' came the quick retort.

'Well, if we had a full team, this game would have been over in two days, instead of three!'

Of course, it was in reference to two days of seven and a half hour playing time, but the point had been made, either way. Suffice to say, it was taken in jest, but it does make you wonder from time to time.

How good would we have been at that time? We will never know.

But at least we had the World Series, which is a lot more than we can say for so many of our countrymen. When we then found out that it had ended, we were very disappointed from a personal point of view. World Series had given us another shot at playing at a higher level, even if it wasn't recognised as Test cricket.

From a wider cricketing perspective, it was obviously the right decision for the game to end the World Series. For one thing, all the best players in the world went back to play for their countries, which was imperative for the health of the sport.

Packer, who had revolutionised so much in terms of broadcast and appeal, had a far firmer footing and his Channel Nine is still a powerhouse to this day, a legacy of the risk he took all those years ago. Many of the players involved at the time have also gone on to become synonymous with Channel Nine, even to this day.

And, most importantly, cricketers were rewarded far better than they had been previously, as their value within the game was more appropriately reflected.

World Series Cricket had been short and sharp, but it had certainly left its mark on the game forever.

Chapter 12

A rainbow nation at the end of a political storm

ONCE SOUTH AFRICAN cricket had been isolated from the rest of the world, most of us resigned ourselves to the fact that we would never fly the South African flag on an international stage again. It was a necessary sacrifice, of course, and it was little compared to what the majority of the South African population had suffered during the apartheid regime.

I was to learn a lot more about the injustices in later years, when I went to start coaching kids in some of the most neglected corners of South Africa. It put into perspective just what real loss was, and I still feel deep regret that so many years were taken away from so many people, all because of the colour of their skin.

Once my playing career had wound down, I had to decide what to do with myself, in order to maintain our young family, and also to keep out of my wife's way by twiddling thumbs in the house for too long! Cricket had been good to me, and I had a huge debt of gratitude to Gloucestershire and the people of Gloucester for that.

They had given me a new lease of life during the 70s, and the benefit year that they afforded me in 1976 was generous and very well supported by the entire county. I had always been impressed by players who had received a benefit year from their county, because it meant that their services had gone beyond the call of duty. I certainly didn't expect mine when it happened, and I was pleasantly surprised.

The money that was realised from that season, coupled with the World Series windfall, meant that there were a few options on the table for when I retired. Amongst some of my possessions, I had bought a Rolls-Royce for £28,000 in cash, just before I came back, knowing I could make a decent profit selling it back in South Africa. I knew that it was time to walk away from the game. My body – especially my knee – certainly knew that the game was up, and I could feel going through that 1982 season that it would be my last.

I had started to miss several games due to fitness concerns, and I absolutely hated that. I felt like I was letting the team down, and that I was maybe holding back fitter and younger players who were raring to push on. It had been, in all honesty, a career that I never thought would have gone as far as it did, and I was genuinely chuffed with the experiences and friends that I had made in the game.

Cricket had been everything for me, and there was a quiet sense of 'what next?' when it all ended. There were offers to stay in England and maybe get into coaching or broadcasting, but Maryna and I really did want to go back home and raise our kids in Durban, where we had also grown up. They had led the lives of somewhat nomadic kids, especially during the World Series, and some normal routine would be good for their education, we felt. Leaving long-standing friends who had almost become family in Gloucester and Bristol wasn't easy, but they completely understood. I felt ready to tackle this next phase of my life, even if I wasn't quite so sure what lay in store.

As a family, we were really happy to be back in Durban. We bought a house in La Lucia, just outside Durban, and kept a flat in the city, in Morningside. The kids got into good schools, and it really felt like things were settling down nicely.

Maryna was back in her home city, amongst friends that she had grown up with or played tennis with, and I also had plenty of mates knocking about from Currie Cup cricket. Durban was a perfect fit for us as a family, and I again realised what the saying 'no place quite like home' truly meant. We were content, and there seemed to be quiet optimism that the country was starting to turn in the right direction. More and more, it looked like our kids would grow up in a democracy, and that was very pleasing.

Having potted about with a few horses, and even acted as an agent for the jockey Mace Roberts while he was looking for a new representative, I knew that it was time to get more serious and find something solid to work with for the next few years. I had a decent amount of capital saved from my playing days, but I needed a business environment to make that flourish and to keep us going as a family for many years to come.

I knew that I was completely out of my comfort zone when it came to finances and business deals, but I had friends from our playing days who had made the transition from players into professionals very nicely. I wanted to do the same, and so started looking around for opportunities. As it happened, an old friend of mine from Rhodesia, Martin Benkenstein, had stumbled upon a potential investment of some promise.

Hummel, the Danish sportswear company, were keen to expand their market, and South Africa seemed like a good fit.

They supplied sports kit, and they were looking for partners who would distribute it from a factory in South Africa. The potential was certainly there, especially as the South African club sport culture was still strong. The potential for growth excited me, and I thought it looked very good on paper. I trusted Martin, as you do people that you had shared a dressing room with. He seemed to be dead certain that this would be a lucrative endeavour, and it sort of kept me in the sports world, so I bit.

In hindsight, I shouldn't have been so cavalier, trusting Martin to handle the books and the day-to-day running of the factory. The business soon ran into debt, and as the one who had put up the surety, I became the fall guy.

The banks came in for what was owed to them, and we lost the business. A lot of the stock that we had was simply the wrong sizes, so we couldn't shift it. We had orders coming in, but we couldn't honour them. It was hugely frustrating, and also confusing how we could get so many orders wrong at the same time. The stock we had was shipped back to Hummel, and we assumed that the proceeds of that were put into the big hole of debt that we were suddenly in. Just like that, the supposed empire crumbled as suddenly as it had started up.

Things were about to get significantly worse for me, as I was the name on all the guarantees. The bank took my house in La Lucia, I had to sell my house in the UK, and the Rolls-Royce was also taken, and sold to the highest bidder. I was devastated. I had been incredibly naïve, but I have heard of many sportsmen who have also trusted blindly, and lived to regret the consequences. That is cold comfort.

In hindsight, I should have taken a keener interest in the whole matter, especially given as my entire life savings were invested in the project. The impact of the entire mess hit us hard as a family. It was truly shattering. The life that we had built up in our heads, the plans we had made for the future, were up in smoke. We kept one of the properties, but only because it was not in my name, but in a trust.

The most galling aspect of the whole matter was Martin's attitude. Not once did he offer an apology or an explanation. Not once. John Trickey, a friend of mine through cricket and squash, revealed to me in later years what Martin had chirped to him when it all fell apart. Trickey was also our marketing director in the Hummel venture.

'Now that Procter's done his dosh, he can go out and find some work!'

Martin signed something that said he owed me a significant amount of money, but there is no way I will ever see that again. Of course, the blame was on his doorstep, but there was no way I couldn't shoulder some of it, too. I had been reckless, and paid the ultimate price. Facing my young family in those dark days was tough, but we simply had to start again. Crying over spilt milk was not going to change anything.

The months immediately after the Hummel business fell apart felt like I had hit rock bottom. My entire life's work had disappeared, and we had a young family that was still trying to make sense of it all. It was a tough time for our marriage, too, because money hadn't been an issue prior to that point.

I still look back at those days in the mid-80s as some of the most testing of my entire life. Facing the might of the West Indies suddenly felt like a walk in the park compared to real life problems. I was seriously close to being sequestrated, and the consequences of that would have followed me around for the rest of my life.

I took a long hard look at myself, and decided that I had to go out there and look for a job. There was nothing much going in terms of cricket, at least not in South Africa. The Currie Cup was well stocked for coaches, and I didn't think I would have got a job straight from playing anyway. So, with the help of some friends, I started selling insurance for Sanlam.

It took a few people by surprise, but I was keen to get some money coming in, and the insurance industry in South Africa was still establishing itself. The theory was that the benefits of the product, coupled with a familiar – well, sort of – face, would help convince a few people to jump on. It was tough work, and quite humbling in the first few months. I felt completely out of my comfort zone, and was learning things that were second nature to those around me.

Cricket had always provided all the answers for me before, so this was fresh territory. I had to keep at it, and I think I did start getting better at the job. But, despite my new-found enthusiasm, I still missed the game. I thought once I stopped playing, I may change priorities, but I missed everything about it. I missed the dressing room, the banter and the crazy road trips that we took to get to matches.

I certainly didn't miss the strain on my body, though. I still felt that I had a lot to offer the game, considering my experience as a player and as a captain. So, when the chance to take over as director of cricket for the Orange Free State came up in the 1988/89 season, I jumped at it. They were a union that was on the up, and had just won promotion to the A division.

The dressing room was full of talent, too. The overseas players, for one thing, were some of the finest men to ever grace South African cricket. Sylvester Clarke was an immense character, a winner and a man unafraid of a challenge. Alongside him was Allan Lamb, formerly of England fame, but now a vital cog in the Free State machine. Alvin Kallicharran was another fantastic pro, and many of the players in Bloemfontein would later take huge lessons from the giant Franklyn Stephenson.

The three West Indians had taken considerable flak back home for coming to South Africa as part of the rebel tour in 1983. Many of their countrymen have never forgiven them, even to this day, because they considered the rebel tour as a show of support for the apartheid government. It was a tense time, for sure, and I can only imagine what they went through. That is the biggest problem with politics and sport; there are, ultimately, no winners. Though Clarke and Kallicharran were personae non gratae back home, they were immense for several years in South African cricket.

I had always liked the idea of an overseas pro in the dressing room. That wasn't just because I had been one on Gloucestershire's books, either! There is an incredible amount of knowledge that comes with a pro. Usually, they are the most experienced in the dressing room, and the up and coming players look to them for inspiration.

But, more than that, they are an infinite source of wisdom. The right pro can turn many a promising cricketer into a great first-class player, and even an international. One only has to look at the incredible work that the late, great Malcolm Marshall did in Natal. The way Shaun Pollock, Lance Klusener, Dale Benkenstein and the rest of that squad grew in his shadow was incredible. He set standards, and they duly followed. So, having the likes of Lamb and Clarke in the shed was very exciting for me.

I must say, the Free State Cricket Union met me more than halfway in terms of the working arrangement. They understood that I had a young family that I didn't particularly want to uproot again. So, the deal was that I was up there every other week, and would come up for the Currie Cup matches and stay the weekend. It also helped me that the union had just been promoted, so there was a lot they were still adjusting to.

As it was, it didn't take long for us to make our presence felt. In the first game back in the top league, we hosted Eastern Province (EP), at the Varsity Ground. There was a massive crowd of students, whose singing and cheering left us in no doubt that they had added something stronger to their Coca-Colas. They were so chuffed to have top-class cricket to enjoy, and that first match was certainly worth missing a few lectures for.

After a magnificent fightback, led by Lamb, we required around 30 runs to beat the mighty EP, in our first match back amongst the elite. The only problem was that we only had four overs to do it in, and the visitors had big Rod McCurdy, the former Australian fast bowler in their ranks, with a new cherry in his mitts. The last thing he was going to do was give us the victory on a platter.

As our boys came back to the changing room, having bowled out EP in the third innings, I jokingly told Clarkie that the game was not over yet, and he might have to go out and hit the winning runs. Clarkie had bowled us back into the game with a magnificent spell of fast bowling, and he must have thought his shift was done. The joke turned out to be a little closer to the truth than I expected, because we lost a few wickets – including a crazy run-out – in the mad dash for runs, and suddenly we only had one ball left, and still needed five runs to win.

Clarke, who had thankfully stayed in his whites, had just walked out to the middle, and was in no mood to waste time. McCurdy and skipper Kepler Wessels took a while trying to set the perfect field. The field they set strongly suggested that a short ball was coming up, with a couple of guys out on the hook. As it was, if McCurdy conceded four runs, the match would have ended in a tie. But, he hadn't reckoned on Clarke going with all guns blazing. McCurdy bowled one back of a length, and Clarke responded by smashing it straight over his head, beyond the sight screen, and that was all she wrote!

It felt like we had won a cup final, and we celebrated our win appropriately that night. As it worked out, I was only in the Free State set-up for one season, due to the travel demands being too much. But, in that season alone, we also had some very good youngsters come through, which I was proud of. Amongst a good bunch, there was a tearaway by the name of Allan Donald, who was wild and wiry, but full of speed. Little did we know that in a matter of a few summers, he would be wearing the green and gold of his country, united at long last, making sure that everyone knew the name 'White Lightning'.

The following season, I was given the chance to be director of cricket a little closer to home, at Natal. It was a homecoming of sorts, and a lot more practical in terms of logistics. Again, it lasted just the one season, but it was another season full of great memories. Natal sport was enjoying a revolution at the time, headed by their rugby side, the Banana Boys.

The wicketkeeper of the side, Errol Stewart, somehow managed to play provincial rugby and cricket – a phenomenal feat, and one that was only possible in those days, when there were clearly defined seasons for summer and winter sport. Errol had to be very well organised, especially at the point when the seasons overlapped, but he somehow managed it. It was little surprise that he was also pretty sharp, and went on to become successful in the corporate world. In recent years, he has been a national selector, one who was respected by players and the media alike, because he has definitely seen it all.

Another great character in the dressing room at Kingsmead at the time was little Jonty Rhodes, who had emerged from Maritzburg College, a school steeped in sporting history. Rhodes was the ultimate energy bunny, and was a hockey star, good enough to be an international cap, too. He used his low centre of gravity to terrific effect in the field, and he was part of the revolution in fielding for world cricket. Long before his iconic run-out of Inzaman in the 1992 World Cup, we could see that he had the very rare ability to change a match purely by the pressure he put on batsmen.

He made the backward point position his own, and his aggressive running between the wickets also put untold pressure on fielders who were stunned by the audacity of this youngster charging around everywhere. Rhodes also used his hockey background for his batting, and he happily swept anything that he could. Though he didn't quite make the runs that a specialist batsman should, he saved at least 30 in the field, and he lifted bowlers and the team with his stunning all-round fielding.

As I got more comfortable with the position, I was given a fresh challenge to be the director of cricket at Northamptonshire. Allan Lamb had gone back to his county, and they were in the market for a director. Allan kindly put my name forward, on the back of our working relationship in Bloemfontein, and the board made me an offer. It was great to be back in county cricket, even if it was slightly unusual to not be at Gloucestershire, my home for so many years.

But, even as we settled into the start of the season, I had been made aware by my good friend Ali Bacher that there was something bubbling in South Africa, and there was growing optimism that we may yet return to international competition. The release of Nelson Mandela in 1990 had been long overdue and, from a sporting perspective, it opened doors that many of us feared would remain closed for a lot longer.

Any sort of return would depend on the country becoming one, of course, and we all owe a significant debt of gratitude to not only Mr Mandela and his magnanimity, but also the incredible passion of the late sports minister, Steve Tshwete. I fondly remember in the manner in which he was depicted in that wonderful picture, with Peter Kirsten, celebrating our World Cup win over Australia in Adelaide.

Tshwete was part of the team, and for all the right reasons. Politics and sport are often at odds with each other, but his determination for us to get to the World Cup, as well as other sports to get to their highest stages, showed how much could be done when power was combined with passion. For him, getting the South African flag there meant as much as it did to us, because it meant we were back in the community, a country again.

Between Tshwete and Ali Bacher came the merging of the South African Cricket Union (SACU) and South African Cricket Board (SACB), which were divided along racial lines. In June 1991 they became the United Cricket Board of South Africa (UCBSA), which was to later become Cricket South Africa. Over the past decade, Cricket South Africa has done a lot to recognise the achievements of those who couldn't fully represent our country during isolation.

They present Heritage Blazers to players of the past, and it was an especially proud moment for me when I received mine during the Boxing Day Test between England and South Africa in 2015. That it happened at Kingsmead, in front of a lot of friends and family, made it all the more special. Some might say that it's a meaningless exercise, but I and many others were genuinely moved. Recognition, even belated, confirms that the hard yards that we all took, even on different paths, were worth it, ultimately.

One thing that I feel conflicted about is the line that Cricket South Africa have drawn on players from before 1991, when they pass away. On one hand, I understand that they want to make a fresh start, but you also can't change your past. You learn from it, and you endeavour not to repeat the mistakes from before.

But honouring past players, which teams around the world still do to this day, is something I feel quite strongly about. Recently, when I was analysing the Proteas' 2016 series in Australia, as a guest for Kwese Sports, we noticed that the players were all wearing black armbands. Trevor Goddard, the former South African captain had passed away, so I was asked if they were honouring him as a former captain.

I figured they must be, and thought it was a great gesture, and perhaps Cricket South Africa had a change of heart with regards to their policy on former players. But, as play went on, it emerged that the black armbands were to mark the anniversary of Phil Hughes' death, the Australian batsman who had been killed on the field two years previously. I am fully behind honouring Hughes in that fashion, as his untimely death was a shock to all. The nature of his death – felled by a bouncer – has seen even greater emphasis on safety, with helmets reinforced. His death was a sad moment for the game, especially for one so young and promising.

In the midst of that sorrow, I found it very sad that the passing of a former captain of ours went by with precious little mention. To my mind, it came across like the team was only honouring an Australian, and not one of their own, who had passed on that very day. I know that it is a stance that Cricket South Africa have taken with regards to players of the past, but I personally don't agree with it. I think captains, in particular, should be acknowledged when they pass, and I don't think it would reflect on Cricket South Africa in any negative way. Their initiative with the Heritage Blazers has been warmly received, and I think most people would appreciate seeing players of the past, on both sides of the divide, acknowledged when they pass away.

As things started to take shape back in 1991, Ali contacted me to give me a heads up. He had been in serious conversations with cricket leaders around the world, and felt quietly confident that the ICC would vote us back into international cricket at their annual meeting at Lord's. Ali asked if I would be interested in becoming the team coach, because he was already trying to see if there was any way we could set up fixtures.

I was taken aback, genuinely. To this day, I can still remember the phone call from Ali when it was finally confirmed that we were back in. I was in Northampton, and he was at HQ, Lord's. He was beyond chuffed, emotional even, and I wasn't far off. I was still in shock, processing the whole thing. We were back in international cricket, back on the map. It had been a long, long journey, but the likes of Ali, who had seen his reign as captain cut short in 1970, had seen it through, tenaciously fighting and never giving up hope.

Things happened very quickly after that. Ali told me that he had tried his best, but we were too late to be involved in the 1992 World Cup, to be staged in Australia. He told me that there was a very good chance that we would go to India, as Pakistan had pulled out of the tour, and the BCCI were still keen to honour the fixture list.

And so, the wheels were in motion for South African cricket again. It very quickly dawned on me that we had to start thinking about a squad to take to India, where none of us had played before. Ali, in his role as team manager, had already made significant strides, and was in daily contact with his Indian counterparts. Though it was a whirlwind period for all involved, South African cricket was in the best possible hands it could be for that period, because Ali cared immeasurably about getting the game back on the map.

Never once did he look back and say that it was a pity it took so long, because he was not that kind of man. His leadership on the field was only seen for a short time, but in the days of re-admission, he showed all the virtues of the captain he was. He never panicked, he never showed any outward strain, but kept on reinforcing the notion that everything was in order, and South African cricket was back on the big stage.

India, with a strong historical connection to South Africa, was our first port of call, and we couldn't wait.

Chapter 13

Selection headaches

THROUGHOUT MY career, I always regarded being a captain as the toughest job in cricket. You had to adapt to the rhythm of the game, inspire your team, and still take care of your business as a player.

I was fortunate in that I was able to contribute with bat or ball, so I had two bites of the cherry, so to speak. I guess having two feathers in the cap, instead of one, also made the selection panel's job a bit easier. All-rounders have become an even bigger deal in the modern game, but it took me becoming a selector to truly appreciate the value of having two-for-one players.

When it came to picking a side, I felt that a captain was perhaps best placed to see what the team required. I was adamant that you had to be on the selection committee as a captain, because you were in the best position to judge your players.

Looking back, I must admit that my line of thinking was perhaps more pertinent to county cricket, where so much of the time is taken up by travelling to the next game, and the luxury of selection meetings and debates wasn't always there. In those circumstances especially, I felt that a captain had a huge role to play.

It was only after I stopped playing, and I eventually got into selecting a team, that I appreciated just how difficult a job it was. Being a convenor meant that you were the one who had to field the questions, and explain why you had gone a certain way.

Not too long after I had been relieved of my duties as a match referee, I was offered the position of convenor for the South African Test side. It was at a time when Graeme Smith's side was just establishing themselves as the leading team in world cricket, with a good blend of experience and emerging talent.

It was an exciting time to be involved in the process and, more often than not, the team picked itself. I soon learnt that the art of being in a selection panel was understanding when to trust a player with one more chance, and to see when they had already had one too many opportunities to turn things around.

The team, the coach and the captain thrive on consistency and a show of faith. It is only natural that they would rather err on the side of an extra chance, instead of axing someone prematurely.

The public, naturally, tend to have a different opinion, and trying to balance those books – without emotion – is the toughest part of being a selector. I would often ask myself how I would react as a captain if I really believed someone was about to turn a corner, and the selection panel already had the axe out.

In many ways, I found that it was much easier on everyone if you didn't get too close to the team. Once you started developing personal relationships, it could easily cloud one's judgement. I also saw what it must have been like dealing with a captain and coach from the other side.

Teams, especially on tour, become like a big family, and the strength of that group lies heavily in being able to withstand outside forces and negative influences. As such, it is important for the team to have an environment that feels secure, where players know that good performances will be rewarded and, more importantly, a bad patch wouldn't be immediately seized upon as an opportunity to get you out of the team.

There is no player in the world who will tell you that it is easy to play with the axe over your head. It is a torturous feeling, and that growing anxiety can also have a negative impact on the team. Everyone wants everyone else to perform, and there can be the danger of sentiment clouding the issue at the highest levels.

We are all humans, after all, and we want to see those close to us bounce back and show the world that they are good enough. This is where a selection panel comes in, and the tough decisions have to be made. It's not fun, and knowing whether or not a big performance is around the corner can never be an exact science. Sometimes, just like captaincy, you get lucky with a punt. Selectors, too, can give a legend one last hurrah, and they find the old magic again.

Of course, history will tell us that there are also many other examples of one too many chances sometimes, where all the signs were there that a player needed a break, but it was just too hard to cut the cord.

That side of it, dropping people and taking a team in a new direction, usually comes into it when the team is in transition or turmoil. Winning teams tend to pick themselves, and take a lot of the strain that comes with picking a team away. Funnily enough, winning even allows terms like rotation and players being rested to come into play.

You won't hear of anyone being happy to be rotated when a team is on the back foot, because they know that getting back in may be tough. All of these things are just a part of the considerations of a selector, and I found the role to be mostly enjoyable, with a few awkward episodes along the way.

Coming into the set-up in late 2008 meant that I immediately went back to Australia, where I had endured such a testing period just a year before. Happily, I wasn't in the firing line this time, and my chief responsibility was to help pick a side that could finally break our hoodoo Down Under.

Central to our plans was the form of our batting giants up front. Graeme Smith and Jacques Kallis were respected around the world, and they both had the look of men determined to bring that series home. They had both suffered some big losses at the hands of Australian sides, and they must have felt that 2008/09 was their best chance to exact revenge.

Smith, especially, was immense during that period of time. Leadership comes in different forms, but you couldn't mistake his presence. He had taken on the job from a very young age, but he had snatched it with both hands. Whenever he was making runs in the middle, the team was relaxed and confident, and he had a massive tour with the bat that year.

I was to later learn that he never made a Test match century in vain. Whenever Graeme Smith reached three figures, South Africa never lost a Test match. Surely, those kinds of stats would have reached the opposition, too, so they knew that they had to get him early.

Another trait of Smith's was his ability to shield his team from the spotlight. He took it upon himself to take the brunt of the press engagements, and always looked to be on the front foot with the press. The Australian press can be ruthless, and they would always target a visiting captain if they felt he was a threat. Smith got his retaliation in first, and made sure his side didn't take a backward step.

When we arrived in Australia, our plans were changed by circumstances, when Ashwell Prince was injured in the build-up to the first Test in Perth. Prince was the ideal man to have on a tough tour, because he didn't give an inch. He had shown his class during the trip to England earlier that year, with a terrific hundred at Headingley, which played a massive part in securing that match and, ultimately, the series.

Losing him was a blow, but there was depth in the squad. A very talented youngster from Western Province, JP Duminy, had been waiting in the wings for a few years in the Test plans, so it made sense that he would step into the breach.

The other consideration had been to play four seamers on the bouncy Waca wicket. We had Lonwabo Tsotsobe, the tall left-arm seamer, in reserve, but Paul Harris had been pivotal in the attack for a year, and both Graeme Smith and Mickey Arthur were very sure that we needed his control in between the bursts from Dale Steyn, Makhaya Ntini and Morne Morkel.

Of course, history will tell that those decisions came off, with Harris playing his restricting role to perfection, and Duminy being there on the final day, scoring a half-century to see the side chase down over 400.

It was an incredible day, and you could feel the belief swell in the dressing room. The elusive series victory in Australia was one more win away, and the locals were ruffled. Smith had made a ton, Kallis had been attacking, and youngsters AB de Villiers and Duminy had stood up to the pressure.

Smith and coach Mickey Arthur were doing a sterling job, and it was the easiest selection meeting that preceded the second Test, on Boxing Day at the MCG.

'Same again, gentlemen,' or words to that effect was the underlying message as we arrived for the second Test. The comfort that comes with a team that picks itself ahead of a big Test or tournament is definitely one of the better feelings for a selector.

Ashwell Prince wasn't ready to return to action yet, but the way that JP Duminy had handled his first assignment spoke volumes about his character. We all know what he then did in the following Test, with his brilliant 166 lifting the team up from the dead, and turning an entire match around.

Winning the series in that fashion was hugely satisfying for the team, and it was quite revealing to see how the Australian media and public got on the back of their selection panel, demanding changes. The glory days couldn't last forever, of course, but they had never foreseen being 2-0 down to the South Africans.

The team went to Sydney in a bubbly mood, with the chance to get a clean sweep, and really put the seal on a wonderful trip. The cricket gods must have thought we were having too much of a good time with all of this, and Graeme Smith was struck a fearsome blow by Mitchell Johnson, the Aussie left-arm tearaway.

Smith had broken a finger, but he still found the courage to try and save that third and final Test match on the final evening. It was crazy that he and Makhaya Ntini came within ten balls of doing just that, and was a testimony to his courage and leadership that he was willing to bat with one good hand.

Of course, in the back of our minds was the worry if Smith would be able to play in the return series, to be held in February. We had a bit of time to get him fit, but Ashwell Prince was still not ready. We had barely had injuries to worry about, and now two of our toughest customers in the batting department had suffered broken fingers.

Smith was, of course, more than just an opening batsman. His leadership style had allowed South Africa's Test side to finally scale the mountain to number one in the rankings, and he had won the respect of world cricket in the process. His record away from home was incredible, but he was also very keen for touring sides to find South Africa a tough place to visit.

Luckily for us, Smith did recover, and was ready to start the Test series in February 2009. Our bone of contention was around Ashwell Prince, who was also fit again. He had been the incumbent before getting struck in practice, and then JP Duminy had grabbed the chance with both hands.

It was an incredibly tough decision, but we left Prince out of the squad for the first two Test matches. It was a long and tough debate, but we felt that we couldn't ignore Duminy's run of form at that point, and asked a rightfully disappointed Prince to go back to the domestic game to get some runs and time in the middle.

You can imagine the chaos when Smith was hit on the hand in the second Test at a lively Kingsmead, again by the charging Johnson. We were already 1-0 down in the series, and the late Phil Hughes' runs meant that we had an even deeper hole to try and dig ourselves out of.

Duminy was still making runs, but he was stranded on 73 as the Aussies burnt through the tail in our first dig. With Smith unable to bat, we crumbled, and the euphoria of Melbourne, just a few months before, was replaced by serious concerns about the make-up of our team for the final Test in Cape Town.

Prince had to come back, with runs in the domestic four-day series, and Smith injured. He still wasn't happy with the manner in which his return had materialised, and we also asked him to come back as an opener, and not in the middle order. We felt that his technique could do well against the Australian new ball, even though he hadn't batted up the order in a very long time.

With the series gone, we also felt it was the right time to replace Neil McKenzie. He had been shifted to the top of the order, and had performed reasonably in Asia and England. But the faster pitches and bowling of Australia had been tough on him, as popular as he was in the dressing room. The tough decisions were seldom popular, of course.

Imraan Khan, the heaviest scorer on the domestic scene that year, was given a Test debut. The Durban High School product was a long-time friend of Hashim Amla, but had also played a lot of representative cricket with several players in the squad. He was in the best form of his life, so we felt comfortable with him coming in at the top of the order.

The final issue for us was the make-up of our attack. Morne Morkel had been very low on wickets, even though he had done a reasonable job in support of Ntini and Steyn in Australia. I felt that he needed some time away from the pressures of international cricket, so he could regain some confidence and form.

With all the changes in personnel, Mickey Arthur wasn't too keen on another change. But, it was essential that we strike with the ball, and Morkel had found little joy with Phil Hughes in particular, who seemed to enjoy his shorter length.

In Australia, he had got nine wickets at a touch over 40 apiece. In the two return Tests, he had taken six wickets at about 50 runs apiece, so his numbers were certainly not doing him any favours, either.

Breaking the news to Morkel was not very easy, because he was also desperate for a final chance to get it right. He was quite emotional, and I could understand the pride in performance that he had. To make matters worse, he was going to be replaced in the side by his brother, Albie Morkel, the hard-hitting all-rounder who was gaining a fearsome reputation.

It must have been an especially bitter sweet moment for the Morkel family that week, but we had to take our emotions out, and pick a side that we felt could best serve us that week at Newlands.

We still had to pick a captain, mind you. Ashwell had done it before when Smith was last injured, but he made it clear that he already had enough on his plate. It was a comeback Test match, and he was suddenly opening the batting, and feeling the need to almost prove himself again. He had a point, and we eventually asked Jacques Kallis to deputise in the leading role.

After what felt like a very long week, in the lead-up to that final Test in Cape Town, things actually turned out rather well. Prince came out and made a defiant 150 as an opener, showing that class really is permanent. It couldn't have been easy for him, and I still wonder if the events of that summer hastened his decision to go and try his hand at county cricket.

We won the match, but the series itself belonged to Australia, and Mitchell Johnson in particular. The Aussies had exacted immediate revenge for their 2-1 loss earlier that summer, and just as we had left them in a state of disarray, we ended our Test series with a lot of questions to ask ourselves.

I was relieved when the summer was finally over. I obviously hadn't expected it to be easy, because it is international sport, after all. But I also hadn't reckoned on the fortunes fluctuating quite so dramatically, and having to make so many decisions around emotionally charged situations, all in one summer.

There were more challenges to come down the road, but the experiences of that first few months of the job taught me a heck of a lot. I made a point of not reading the papers too much, in much the same way that I didn't try and associate too much with the team.

It is easy to get influenced if you put yourself in a position to be, and I was quite happy to keep to myself and the rest of the selection panel. Looking back, I realised just how much the game had changed from the 1992 World Cup, when I had first sat in on selection meetings.

Despite all the changes to the game, one constant is that every single player wants to play at every opportunity for their country. You can't blame players for that because it is a short career, after all. Having played myself, I completely understood that desperation to be on the park whenever the call came.

Having dealt with the Duminy/Prince issue, and then having to break the news to Morne Morkel later in that first summer, I felt that I was getting used to the pressures of the job. I was getting used to the way that Graeme Smith and Mickey Arthur thought and felt, which played a big part in selection, in my opinion. Your coach and captain are far closer to everything, and the sooner you understand them better, the smoother the job will be.

It had been going along smoothly, until England visited our shores in 2009/10. After what had transpired in 2008, when Smith had secured South Africa's first series win in England since

1965, the old enemy was bound to come back hard at us. What resulted was a bizarre series, one that we ultimately shared, but we really ought to have won comfortably.

Graham Onions became the most celebrated number 11 in history, saving two Test matches by seeing off the final over on day five. For your last batsman to do that once is memorable, but twice is just crazy. There was a massive reaction from the public, all questioning how we hadn't managed to bowl out the last man.

Makhaya Ntini was given the responsibility of the last over at Centurion, but he couldn't find a way past Onions' defence. Though that single over didn't result in him being dropped, he increasingly had the look of a man who was losing his powers. What he had achieved in his career couldn't be emphasised or repeated often enough. He was South African cricket's first black superstar, and he had carried the mantle single-handedly, for a decade.

His penultimate Test, at Centurion, was his 100th, an incredible achievement for any individual. Makhaya was given a rousing reception, and Cricket South Africa marked the occasion with the necessary pomp and ceremony. There was not a single South African who wasn't proud of what Makhaya Ntini had achieved.

And yet, by the end of that first Test of the series, after failing to close out the win, people were questioning how much more Ntini had in the tank. His biggest attribute had always been an ability to go wide of the crease, and then get the occasional ball to hold up, nicking off key scalps. Of course, Ntini's other tremendous strength was an engine that seemed capable of bowling forever.

We probably took him for granted, but all the greats eventually start to diminish. The same had happened to Allan Donald and Shaun Pollock before him, and the end looked to have come for Ntini, too. Of course, given the dynamics, it still wasn't the easiest decision in the world. We gave him the second Test, over Boxing Day, to get back on track, but he was again our poorest bowler on show.

Along with Dale Steyn, we looked to Makhaya to be our strike bowler, but he was ineffective, and also leaked runs. His analysis at Kingsmead was an unflattering 0-114 from 29 overs. We lost that Test, as Graeme Swann spun a web to claim nine wickets in the match, to continue a terrible run of form in Durban for our side. It was getting increasingly clear what had to be done, but Makhaya didn't see it the same way.

He felt that he deserved better as a senior player, and was not very happy at all to be dropped midway in the series. It was a tense time, not least because we were still trying to get back in the series. The public fallout was also something to consider. Makhaya Ntini was a hero to millions of children, right across the country. His story was the blueprint for what could be achieved, but the champion had lost his punch.

We tried to sit him down and explain that we could do something similar to what Shaun Pollock had when he retired, where his final ODI series became an extended national farewell and a sincere thank you to an icon. We felt that Makhaya could bow out in similar circumstances, and the public could be given a heads up.

He would have been seen as going out on his terms, and giving the country his own, personal thanks, too. But he was adamant that he wasn't done yet, and that he was being used as a scapegoat for the loss in Durban. Things became quite heated, but all we could do as a selection panel was to remind ourselves that our job was to pick a team that we felt could win the next match, and put emotions aside.

As it turned out, that Durban Test match was to be Makhaya's last. He finished on 390 Test wickets, which was a terrific return, and placed him second behind Shaun Pollock on our all-time list.

He had also been part of some serious wins around the world, and had become as much of an ambassador for South Africa as any of our leading sportsmen.

But cricket, and all professional sports for that matter, evolve over time, and some of the hardest decisions involve those players and personalities that become larger than life. In a perfect world, Makhaya Ntini would have retired on his own terms, in a blaze of glory. But sport doesn't always work like that.

Over the years, there have been hundreds of Test cricketers, and very few get the luxury of going out at the right time. The fairytale doesn't always materialise in elite sport, and my stint as a national selector re-emphasised that point to me.

I was proud to have been associated with another significant passage of South African cricket, one which saw the Test side become the best in the world. By the time that 2011 World Cup came around, I knew I was coming to the end of the journey. We went with what we felt was a strong squad for the conditions, and we again looked well on the way to competing for the title.

I still can't put my finger on what happens to our side in the World Cup, having seen all of them at close quarters. In 1992, I was obviously the team coach. In 1996 and 1999, I was commentating for the world feed. In 2003, even as a match referee, I watched with bated breath like every South African, and still can't believe that rain and (not so) simple mathematics again cost us.

In 2007, I was again a match referee, as we were blown away by the Australians in a quarter-final. So, watching on in 2011, I thought we had covered our bases, especially with the selection of Imran Tahir, the Pakistan-born leg-spinner. He had married a lady from Durban, and had gone through the necessary procedures to qualify.

There was initially some debate around the country about playing someone who was born outside of South Africa, but Imran

Tahir soon won the sceptics over with his boundless enthusiasm and pride for his adopted country.

I saw no issue with that. After all, it is the 21st century, and there are rules in place to ensure that those who decide to adopt another country serve the necessary time to prove that they are really committed.

For the growth of the game, I would far rather see a good player be part of a national team somewhere in the world, because that is all part of growing our sport. Smaller teams like Scotland, Holland and Ireland have done very well with the help of imports, and those small nations have even started causing upsets at major tournaments.

Of course, we saw Tahir as a match-winner, and he had a full bag of tricks at his disposal. He had already played around the world in first-class competitions, and everyone within the team took to him immediately. His energy was infectious, though the team soon knew better than to try and keep up with him when he celebrated a wicket.

Ultimately, that World Cup campaign again fell short, as we unravelled to a dogged New Zealand side. The inevitable c-word came up, and I guess it will always be part of our game until we win one of these World Cups.

The most recent World Cup, in 2015, saw South Africa fall just short, again to New Zealand. But many of us watched on with a bemused expression when we saw the teams for that semi-final in Auckland. Kyle Abbott had been brilliant in the quarter-final win over Sri Lanka, and cricket sense dictated that he had to be a shoo-in for the next game.

So, it was a shock to all that he was suddenly on the bench, and Vernon Philander was playing instead. In the days that followed, it was disconcerting to hear growing rumours that there had been political interference, which insisted that Philander had to play instead of Abbott.

Cricket South Africa have stubbornly refuted these allegations, of course, but it still makes no sense as a pure cricketing decision. Philander had barely played, and Abbott was in the form of his life with the new ball, and he was a very good finisher at the death. I was later informed that Mike Hussey, who was working as the batting consultant for South Africa, said the mood had never been better at dinner before the squad was announced. There was real belief and excitement in the group, and then that was instantly deflated by the shock of the team chosen.

There were all sorts of rumours, some of which still circle today, about how the players took it. Some say that AB de Villiers didn't want to play, and that even Philander didn't want to play. As ever, the biggest mess is left for the players to clean up, and it is them that you really feel sorry for.

Abbott has since packed his bags to play county cricket as a Kolpak player, and you cannot blame him. Cricket is a short career, and there are even less certainties these days. He must have been gutted on the morning of that semi-final, and Philander would not have felt much better.

It reminded me of a similar situation on 2001/02, when Percy Sonn, then president of the United Cricket Board, waded in and demanded that Justin Ontong play instead of Jacques Rudolph in the third Test against Australia. Rudolph, a white player, had been picked to play that third Test, but Sonn insisted that Ontong had to play instead. Both of them were young men, with plenty of talent, but they were suddenly political pawns. To put into perspective how deeply it affected them, they were both in tears at the situation, one which they had done nothing to create. It's always the innocent parties that suffer most.

There was, naturally, a huge reaction in South Africa, and Gerald Majola, then CEO of the United Cricket Board, and I had to talk to the team when we arrived for the one-day part of the tour, and try to put them at ease. It was clear that there was a lot of emotion within the dressing room, and they were in no shape to face the best team in the world. Graham Ford, the coach, would later say that he 'never wanted to go down that road again', which was telling in itself.

The team then had a sudden change in fortunes, winning the World Series competition involving New Zealand and Australia, to everyone's pleasant surprise. Ford, a team man to the hilt, said that the talk that we had with the team was instrumental in allowing the players to focus purely on their cricket, and it was really no coincidence that they started playing with confidence again, once everyone knew where they stood. It was the first ever trophy we had won in Australia.

For all his detractors in later years, Gerald Majola was very good for South African cricket. The players respected him for it and, as convenor of selectors, I was also very appreciative of his support.

I have always insisted that sport and politics should never mix, and very little has made me change that opinion over the years. I agree completely with transformation, but there has to be very clear stipulation, so that everyone knows exactly what is going on.

Incredibly, the United Cricket Board took a decision to scrap quotas just six months after the Ontong/Rudolph debacle, back in July 2002. Percy Sonn himself said that they felt that the likes of Ntini, Prince and Ontong playing at the highest level had shown that transformation was happening in the national team.

Of course, the system never really went away, and in recent years, there has been a far clearer guideline, with a quota of six non-white players expected to be chosen in each South African team that takes the field. That means a maximum of five white players.

For a player, there cannot be anything worse than playing and not being sure if you are there for purely cricketing reasons.

Merit should be the only criteria, and there are more than enough players who have earned the right to play for South Africa, without the label of being a quota player. I think it takes away from their own talents, which is completely unfair.

One could argue that by having a quota policy, then team selection cannot be purely on merit. If it was on merit, there would be no need for the quota in the first place.

One day – sooner rather than later, I hope – we can watch a multi-racial South African team, which doesn't need quota guidelines, and they can go on and win a World Cup for all South Africans. I find it truly baffling that 1992 still remains as the closest we got to going all the way, but I still retain hope that we will live to see that day. There is so much talent and passion in this country, and one hopes that the current crop will get over the line in 2019, and erase the pain of that 1999 meltdown, as well as everything that happened in 2015.

Chapter 14

Friends in the game

THE ONE enduring factor about cricket is that the friends you make in the game tend to last forever. One of the good friends I made in the game is Garry Sobers, or 'Sobey' as I would affectionately grow to call him.

I remember the first time I saw Sobey play, when I was just 16, back in 1963. We were on tour with the South African Schools team, which included Barry Richards and Hylton Ackerman. The West Indies were touring England that year, and we happened to get tickets to the final day's play of the Lord's Test.

As luck would have it, we got a real humdinger, with England holding on for a famous draw, in a match that still could have produced any result going into the final over. Colin Cowdrey, who had broken his arm during the match, had to come out for the last over, but he was at the non-striker's end. The reception that Cowdrey got from the members, as he gallantly strode out to try and do his bit to save the Test, was something special. In fact, I would liken it to the ovation Graeme Smith received in Sydney, when he went out to bat with a broken hand in 2008/09.

David Allen had to see off Wes Hall in the last over, but England were also not completely out of the running for the victory. In the end, they were five short of the Windies' total, but had shared the spoils in a wonderful contest. We were riveted by the whole drama, and the theatre that comes with being at Lord's for a Test match.

Three years later, Lee Irvine, Barry and I were back in England, on a Wilf Isaacs private tour. With his contacts, he managed to get us to clean the kit for the West Indian team after the day's play at the Oval Test match. We were very happy to do so, as it meant rubbing shoulders with the mighty Windies side. We also didn't have the money to get into the ground every day, so cleaning the boots meant going in for free. Naturally, we were very happy with the deal on the table!

Garry Sobers was captain and, like many of the leaders that have come from the islands, he had a considerable presence about him. We would come in at the end of each day's play, and clean boots and pads, revelling in the thrill of being in an international dressing room. We were happy to do whatever odd jobs they handed to us.

We never really said much to Sobey, then, but our friendship would develop greatly over the next few years, on the county scene. I was at Gloucestershire, and he was the main man at Notts. We had some terrific battles, but always in the right spirit.

When the South African tour to England of 1970 was cancelled, there was a big gap in the middle of the English summer. There was a hastily arranged five-match Test series between England and the Rest of the World, to ensure that there was still quality cricket on offer to the public.

For a team that was put together at the last minute, the Rest of the World XI was pretty formidable. Sobey was captain, and he also had Rohan Kanhai, Clive Lloyd and Lance Gibbs from the Windies team. Eddie Barlow, Barry Richards, Graeme Pollock and I were the South African contingent, and played in all five Test matches, while Peter Pollock also featured.

The jovial Farokh Engineer from India and Lancashire was one of our keepers along with Deryck Murray of the West Indies. All in all, we had a cracking team and morale. England had a powerful unit at that time, too, and everyone anticipated a very good series. As it was, we won 4-1, but it was a lot closer than that. A lot hinged on the fourth Test, which we went into 2-1 up. England had to win in order to keep the series alive, and they very nearly did so.

The match provided the very rare occasion of Barry batting at 10, which I doubt he had ever done in his life! He had injured his back on the first day, taking a catch to dismiss Basil D'Oliveira, off my bowling. He hadn't come back on the field for the whole match, but we were now in a bit of a fix, having slipped to 75 for 5, chasing 223 for a series-clinching victory on a Leeds wicket that was turning, and playing up and down. By the time Barry joined me in the middle, we were 183 for 8, still 40 short of the win.

With all due respect to Lance Gibbs, our resident number 11, it was up to Barry and I to save the situation. Barry survived an early appeal for a bat-pad off Don Wilson, and then England resorted to pace. John Snow took the new ball, and Chris Old was providing the support. We managed to stay composed, and slowly inched our way to the target.

It was even more special because it meant we clinched the series. To their credit, England kept on going to the very last, desperate to find a way to keep the series alive. 4-1 was certainly a bit harsh on them, but that series as a whole was a great advert for Test cricket, even though the ICC eventually deemed it was unofficial.

That was a funny one, because Garry had signed up to be captain on the premise that the series was going to be afforded Test status. The ICC then made an about-turn, and it was something that I always found strange.

Much like the World Series, that 1970 series was a terrific display of cricket, with a host of world-class players. How that didn't warrant Test status I will never know. The crowds also turned up in support, and I remember a very partisan crowd at The Oval.

A particular highlight from that series was seeing Graeme Pollock and Garry Sobers in full flow together at the crease. It was a partnership that everyone had craved, but the magic didn't happen until the final match at The Oval. On that day, they added 165 runs together, with Graeme going on to make a century, and Sobey got 79.

Coincidentally, I had a very good series with the bat, and actually ended third on the batting averages behind Sobers and Lloyd. I even managed to score more runs than Pollock and Richards – something that you couldn't say every day, and not something I was likely to repeat! I was obviously thrilled with my return, and it was a fantastic series all round, on and off the field.

The West Indian lads and the South Africans got on so well that we had already discussed the need to get Garry to come over to Southern Africa. Getting him to South Africa was out of the question, given the political climate, but we figured that Rhodesia wouldn't be too much of an issue.

The reason we wanted him to come to Rhodesia was because he was such a fantastic cricketer, and was also such a magnetic personality. An example of his ability was what he did in the first Test of the England–Rest of the World series. He took six wickets bowling pace to rout England for 127, then made 183 with the bat.

As if that wasn't enough, he then took two more wickets bowling spin in the second innings, and a couple of fantastic catches, as we won by an innings. You just couldn't keep him out of the game.

We felt that his visit would provide a major boost to cricket in Rhodesia. I spoke to Alwin Pichanick – who was manager of the

Rhodesia Cricket Union, and would later become president – and he got the wheels in motion.

We got Garry over a few months after that 1970 series, and we even managed to organise a double-wicket competition, with the West Indian legend as the headline act. He was paired with Ali Bacher, and he just about fell over laughing when he saw Ali bowling for the first time. Of course, Ali was never much of a bowler, but he had to do so in the competition. Despite his part-time offerings, he and Garry managed to go all the way and win the competition – and there weren't even any bookies in those days!

Garry took a lot of flak back home for visiting Rhodesia, who had assumed independence from the British Empire. Many people in the West Indies saw his meeting with then Rhodesian president Ian Smith as 'naïve', but Garry had a simple answer for his critics. He was once quoted as saying, 'I try and build bridges, not break them down.'

As one of the great ambassadors of the game, he was simply trying to spread the gospel of cricket, and was trying to do that in every corner of the world. Garry and I have managed to stay in touch for decades, long after we stopped sharing a field. I was most pleasantly surprised when he invited me over to Barbados in 2016, to take part in the celebrations for his 80th birthday.

Barbados is just a wonderful part of the world, and the perfect place to unwind. Of course, it was a fabulous occasion, surrounded by many great cricketing names that we met along the way. The party itself was a week-long affair, with gala dinners, a celebrity cricket match, some golf, and terrific company. The great man never did do half measures!

The friends that I made through the game were not just limited to cricketing circles. Sir Victor Blank, a giant in finance and a great philanthropist, first invited me to one of his and the late Sir David Frost's Wellbeing for Women's charity cricket matches in 1994, when I was still South African coach.

The match is always held at Victor's country manor in Oxfordshire, and it has become one of the great social and fundraising dates on the UK calendar. For many of us, the occasion is a great place to give back to society, as well as to catch up with old acquaintances. Sir Michael Parkinson is a permanent fixture, usually as an umpire, and usually one of Clive Lloyd or myself is the other man in a coat.

Over the years, the likes of Shane Warne, Brian Lara, Sachin Tendulkar, Viv Richards and many other former greats from around the world have come along to do their bit for charity.

I used to play, too, but Chippinghurst Manor is officially the last ground that I ever bowled a ball on. Mind you I was only bowling my off-spin, but I did my knee, and had to go in for my eighth and last knee operation.

Those annual get-togethers, for a wonderful cause, are always a reminder of how lucky we have been to play sport for a living. Seeing so many greats from the game, from the media and the entertainment world also reinforced in me the responsibility that we have as sportsmen or people of profile to highlight the plight of others.

It was probably with that thought at the back of my mind that the idea behind the SAPS Widows and Orphans Fund Golf Day was born. I have always regarded the South African police force in the highest regard, especially given the extreme danger that they put themselves in front of on a daily basis.

There is a lot of negative publicity about our police force, but there are many, many officers who sacrifice their lives in the line of duty for us, as citizens. I was having a drink at Durban North Police Station, as was customary on Fridays back then, and that was when I first mentioned the idea of raising money for the police.

From there, a committee was formed, and it was decided that it would be best to channel the funds raised towards the Widows and Orphans Fund, through an annual golf day that I would put together with the help of the police.

The golf day started out as a small corporate event, with terrific support from sporting personalities. It has blossomed into an extraordinary outpouring of generosity, which fills up two championship courses on one very busy, but most rewarding day each May.

Over the years, I have become good friends with Brigadier Marius van Rensburg, whose incredible effort, along with his organising committee, on an annual basis have seen to it that the golf day runs smoothly and successfully. The golf days themselves wouldn't be the success that they have become without the wonderful support that we enjoy from so many of our corporate friends and sponsors.

I must also add that the support from the wider sporting community in South Africa has been truly humbling. Ian McIntosh, the great rugby legend, has never missed a single golf day, and many of his players have also become permanent fixtures over the years.

There are too many to mention them all, but they include the likes of Andre Joubert, Butch James, John Allan, Wayne Fyvie and Ray Mordt from rugby, as well as Shaun Pollock, Errol Stewart, Lance Klusener, Jonty Rhodes and several friends from my playing days. Barry Richards and Lee Irvine have also lent their support.

Cricket and rugby have always had a close relationship in South Africa, probably because most sportsmen played both codes during their school days. But, the support I have received over the years extends far beyond cricket and rugby.

One of the regular faces at each golf day has been Neil Tovey, the former South African football captain, and a very keen golfer in his own right. Golfers such as the late, great Simon Hobday, Peter Matkovich and Mus Gammon have also played on occasion, along with fellow Rhodesian Brian Murphy. Kevin Shea from the horse-racing fraternity is also a friend of the golf day.

A common thread with so many of the sportsmen that come to these days is that they are always willing to donate memorabilia, which is auctioned off to raise even more funds.

It really is incredible how it all comes together, and the generosity of spirit amongst people from diverse fields and backgrounds is always inspiring. The fact that we have now gone over ten years and continue to grow every year is testimony to a lot of people working hard to secure sponsors and donors, even in these increasingly tough times.

Mount Edgecombe Country Club have become excellent hosts of the event for us for a number of years now, and we often stay deep into the night, reminiscing on previous years, and looking forward to the next one.

The golf days are great days in themselves, but I have always been very keen to give back to the game that gave me so much. Cricket remains as an unattainable to many people in this country, due to a lack of proper facilities and equipment. Of all the sports, it is probably the most expensive to get started in, given all the requirements just to play with a hard ball.

It remains a challenge for government and cricket authorities, but it is one that would be greeted with enthusiasm, I am sure. I say that with certainty because I have been involved in coaching a rural school, on the outskirts of Durban, for the last five years.

My friend Rodney Malamba, a fine cricketer in his day, and I wanted to introduce the game to a school that didn't have the sport as an outlet, and he suggested Ottawa Primary School. It is situated near a township, and a lot of the kids are affected by the ramifications of HIV/AIDS. School, for them, is a way out of those circumstances, even if only for a few hours a day. Some of them also get their only meal of the day at the school.

They didn't have sport, and though that may seem like a foreign concept to some, it is a reality for too many school children in our country. There are no fields, usually, and even when there are, there are no coaches to guide children and ignite a passion for whatever sport they may fancy. It is a vicious circle, but one that must be broken if we are to go forward and provide opportunities as a country.

What Rodney and I wanted to try and do was at least establish a culture of sport for the kids, even on a weekly basis. We went in blind, and we were blown away by the numbers, and the absolute thirst for stimulation within the kids.

Initially we had a sponsor, but that fell away after about 18 months. However, having been involved with the kids and having seen their enjoyment at close quarters, it was impossible to walk away. Having funded it myself for a couple of years, I decided to form a foundation which would formalise the distribution of any funds raised.

After a period of time, when we initially coached 40 to 50 kids a week, we had a call from the school principal. Due to the popularity of the sessions, she was requesting that we maybe could incorporate more pupils into our sessions. Between Rodney and I, we decided that whoever wanted to participate was most welcome.

Just like that, our little clinic – during the kids' physical education class period – mushroomed into an army of kids invading us, all smiling and thriving with being out of class and playing. We take a lot of things for granted, sometimes, but the kids of Ottawa Primary have given me great perspective, even in my advancing years!

We used to coach 40 to 50 kids, but now the whole school is involved, on different days of the week. In total, it is around 1,000 children. Given the high volume of participants – up to 200 kids at a single session – the emphasis has shifted from cricket skills to having fun and stimulating the children. Our mornings there have become a great source of inspiration for me, because it is a chance for Rodney and I to see children being just that; children revelling in an open field, playing with their mates.

Of course, being a sporting environment, some kids will show more promise than others. To be honest, our initial goal had nothing to do with unearthing talent. We just wanted to provide an outlet for energy, using cricket as the vehicle. We can already see that some have taken to the game with a natural flair.

An example of this was on one of our first sessions, when we were introducing these boys and girls to the game. Some still needed help with the basics, but I specifically remember a young girl picking up the bat, and we showed her how to grip it accordingly. One of the others then threw a low full toss at her, and she played a shot through the off side, which stood out because the natural tendency for kids at that age is to swing freely towards the leg side. In the midst of the madness, Rodney and I both saw that shot, and we looked across at each other. We both had goose-bumps, and it again reaffirmed our belief that sports come naturally to some. I am certain that, given the right opportunities, she could have gone on to play the game at a very high level. She was instinctive.

The project has received some media attention, especially when England toured South Africa in 2015/16. Several journalists came to see what it was all about, and the kids were brilliant in their answers. They watch the game, and they want to be the next Rabada, or de Villiers, or de Kock.

There is a passion there, and it must be nourished. Kingsmead Mynahs have also played a massive role in donating kit and food, as well as helping to get two nets put in at the school. I also owe a great deal of gratitude to the English supporters who came over for the 2015/16 season. They donated generously after a Christmas lunch function we had, and those funds ensured that all the kids at the school were fed over the January period, before the government meals kick in.

Indeed, the foundation has seen the project go far beyond cricket. We feel a social responsibility to these children, and we have supplied t-shirts (kindly donated by Vaughan Beddin), blankets, and tried to give them occasional treats. Every January and December, when they don't get food from the government, we have also committed to feeding 1,000 children every school day, to ensure that they don't go without. It is no small task, but one that we have accepted as part of our priorities.

We have taken teachers and children to a match at Kingsmead on three occasions, though we found it incredible that Natal Cricket still insisted that we had to pay full price for each of these children, regardless of their personal circumstances. I have also approached Cricket South Africa on a number of occasions, and it saddens me to say that they have shown scant regard for the welfare of the kids. In fact, in all the years of the foundation being at Ottawa, we have never received one cent, one ball or even a t-shirt in support from the cricketing bodies, which is a terrific shame.

At times, it seems, they miss the bigger picture, even when it is right on their doorstep. To my mind, it is these gestures, from wherever they come, that so many schools around the country need in order to keep the flame of youthful exuberance burning in so many children. A child's simplest pleasure is to play, and watching the hundreds of kids running around at Ottawa has been a great joy.

We have even got to the point where we played our first cricket match, a historic occasion for the school. To see the joy on the kids' faces when they were chosen to represent their school reinforced the fact that what we trying to do is doing its own small bit.

We all know what it is like to be called up to your first representative team, whatever level it may be. To see that on those kids' faces was a great source of pride, and one that we hope to replicate again and again over the next few years.

One thing is for certain, there are so many other Ottawa Primary situations around the country, filled with kids who are just itching for a chance to play and be happy. And, what's more, I think it is at those schools that we may yet find some of the very best players of our future. That is the most exciting part for me, the untapped potential that may be opened up with just a little bit of support and encouragement.

As ever, we live in hope.

Chapter 15

Family

WHEN I look back on my career, I realise that none of it would have been possible without the unflinching support of my wife, Maryna.

I met her in Cape Town, when she was playing a tennis tournament, and I was playing for Natal, back in 1968. Maryna was a terrific tennis player, one of the best in South Africa at the time. She was good enough to go and play the Majors on several occasions, and reached the quarter-finals of the US Open. She also played in a few Federation Cup ties for South Africa.

She was also from Durban, which was very handy of course, given our already hectic schedules. We were both sports professionals, so time was always an issue at that stage. As it was, the courtship was very quick, and we were married by the time I went back to England for the 1969 winter.

They say when you know you know, and we went to the Magistrates' Court in Camperdown, and we then had a proper ceremony a few weeks later in Hillcrest. That year was frenetic, as she was going over to play a few tournaments in Europe, and I was going back to Gloucestershire.

1969 turned out to be the last year on tour for Maryna, as our first son Gregg was born the following year. As a sportsman myself, I was very grateful that she was just as keen to start a family, because the reality was that it would have a bigger impact on her. The manner in which she sorted out the process of moving into our first proper house in England, in Bristol, was also remarkable. As cricketers, we are expected to pitch up, and play season to season, and much of the day-to-day running of the house is taken for granted.

Maryna certainly had a lot on her plate, especially when we were setting up house. She had Gregg, and then the whole organising of the move. But, she took it all in her stride. At that time, with the political climate in South Africa, I was targeted by some fanatical group called the Red Brigade, who were against the apartheid system.

In their mind, we were white South Africans, so they didn't need any further reason. I tried to shield Maryna from much of it, and just tried to carry on. But the secret was out when the cops called her at the house when I was away with the team. They informed her that people were after Mike, and gave her a special number to call if she suspected something. Having not got wind of any of this before, that obviously came as a bit of a shock to the system!

I didn't worry too much about the threats, because there was actually very little you could do, besides calling the police and informing them. There were some hairy moments for Maryna, though, and they always seemed to occur when I was away.

A funny one was when an unusual car parked outside the house, and she was sure that it was 'them'. Cars in England only tended to park in front of your house if they were visiting, but Maryna didn't recognise this particular vehicle. Just as she was about to call the cops, she peered through the curtain, and realised that it was actually a painter!

She was, and remains a fantastically strong character. In 1973, she got the mumps during the season, and we were in the midst of our run to the Gillette Cup Final. I was advised to stay away from home, as I had never had mumps before, and the club didn't want to risk it. So, I was put up in a bed and breakfast, while Maryna had Gregg and the mumps at home. I couldn't go back until she got the all-clear!

She was also there for me when I suffered various injuries and had to have minor surgery, helping me to recuperate. It can't have been easy, but she ran our house like clockwork.

Having children is one of life's great gifts, and we were blessed with Gregg, Tammy and Jessica. Of course, they went wherever I played around the world. Gregg and Jessica were born in South Africa, and Tammy was born in England during the season.

Gregg and Tammy would go wherever we went, so Rhodesia, England and Australia with the World Series were all part of their childhood. While that may sound glamorous to some people, I am sure it was not the easiest thing in the world, especially for Gregg, who had to switch schools every few months, as we chased the sun for cricket seasons.

I have managed to cram a heck of a lot into my career, but I know that half of it would have felt empty without the unflinching support of my wife and children. It wasn't always easy, following me and my dreams around the world, but they certainly made it all the more special by being there – and putting up with me after a bad day on the field!

Life has a funny way of going full circle, and these days, it is Maryna who has found a new lease of life, working in property. The kids have given us grandkids, and obviously the travel bug that got me must have bitten them from a young age, because they are spread around the world!

Gregg remains in Durban, but Tammy is in America – along with three grandkids that are growing up very fast. Jessica, meanwhile, is now living in the UK. We try and visit them as often as we can.

For all the accolades, man of the match awards and the memories that the game has given me, my family remains my most prized possession.

Appendices

Test match record against Australia

Year	Test	Venue	Runs	Overs	Maidens	Wickets	Runs	
1966/7	3rd Test	Kingsmead 1st inngs	1	14	2	3	27	
		2nd inngs	–	29,1	7	4	71	
	4th Test	Wanderers 1st inngs	16	18	7	4	32	
		2nd inngs	–	17	6	2	38	
	5th Test	St Georges Park 1st inngs	0	15,1	3	2	36	
		2nd inngs	–	16	3	0	59	
			Ave: 5,66					
1966/7 Series			17	109,2	28	15	263	Ave: 17,53
1969/70	1st Test	Newlands 1st inngs	22	12	4	2	30	
		2nd inngs	48	17	4	4	47	
	2nd Test	Kingsmead 1st inngs	32	11	2	2	39	
		2nd inngs	–	18,5	5	3	62	
	3rd Test	Wanderers 1st inngs	22	21	5	3	48	
		2nd inngs	36*	14	8	3	24	
	4th Test	St Georges Park 1st inngs	26	25,1	11	3	30	
		2nd inngs	23	24	11	6	73	
			Ave: 34,43					
1969/70 Series			209	143	50	26	353	Ave: 13,58
Test Record			Ave: 25,11					
			226	252,2	78	41	616	Ave 15,02

Miscellaneous South African Records

Equalled World Record of C.B. Fry and D.G. Bradman in scoring 6 hundreds in successive innings:

119 v. Natal 'B'	Bulawayo
129 v. Transvaal 'B'	Salisbury
107 v. Orange Free State	Bloemfontein
174 v. North-Eastern Transvaal	Pretoria
106 v. Griqualand West	Kimberley
254 v. Western Province	Salisbury

Fast Scoring
In scoring 155 in 130 minutes for Western Province v. Australians at Cape Town 1969-70, he scored 9 sixes in the innings including 5 sixes off successive balls in one over from A.A. Mallett. He went from 100 to 150 in only 12 minutes.

Hundred in both innings of a match:
114 and 131 for Rhodesia v. International Wanderers at Salisbury 1972-73. The first time this feat has been performed by a Rhodesian batsman.

Best bowling performance:
9-71 for Rhodesia v. Transvaal at Bulawayo 1972-73 – established the following records:
(i) his own career best bowling analysis.
(ii) the best ever bowling analysis for Rhodesia.
(iii) the best ever bowling analysis against Transvaal.
(iv) the best ever bowling analysis at Bulawayo.
(v) the best bowling analysis of the 1972-73 South African season.
Note: 8 of the 9 wickets were taken when he changed to bowling off-breaks.

500 runs and 50 wickets in a season

1971-72	695 runs	52 wickets
1972-73	870 runs	60 wickets

This feat has only been accomplished 7 times – M.J. Procter is the only player to have done so twice.

His 59 wickets in the 1976/7 season is the most wickets ever taken in a Currie cup season.

During the 1977 English season Mike Procter became the highest South African wicket taker of all time, surpassing C.B. Llewellyn's record of 1013 wickets.

Mike Procter – 1st Class Career Statistics 1965 - 1981

Statistics compiled by Peter Sichel.

Year	Team	Matches	Inn.	N.O.	Runs	H.S.	Ave.	100	50	Catches	Runs	Wkts.	Ave.	10w	5w	B/B
1965	G.L.	1	1	0	69	69	69.00	–	1	–	10	0	–	–	–	–
1965/6	Natal/South	7	10	2	410	129	51.25	1	4	6	427	17	25.11	–	–	4/19
1966/67	S.A./Natal/S.A. XI	9	13	0	208	51	16.00	–	1	7	766	49	15.63	1	1	7/25
1967/8	Natal	6	10	1	338	84	37.55	–	3	5	572	29	19.72	1	3	6/37
1968	G.L.	24	40	1	1167	134	29.92	3	6	9	1218	69	17.65	–	2	6/43
1968/9	Natal/S.A. Games	8	13	1	182	42	15.16	–	–	5	744	32	23.25	–	1	5/89
1969	G.L.	25	39	4	562	52	16.05	–	2	33	1623	108	15.02	1	6	7/65
1969/70	S.A./W.P.	9	15	1	532	155	38.00	2	–	6	717	45	15.93	–	1	6/73
1970	G.L./Rest of World	20	33	7	934	115	35.92	1	5	16	1398	65	21.50	–	2	6/38
1970/1	Rhodesia Rest of S.A.	8	8	0	956	254	119.50	6	–	9	435	27	16.11	–	1	5/8
1971	G.L.	24	43	4	1786	167	45.79	7	6	27	1232	65	18.95	1	2	5/45
1971/2	Rhodesia	10	19	2	695	107	40.88	1	5	8	833	52	16.01	1	3	7/32
1972	G.L.	19	33	3	1219	118	40.63	3	7	13	960	58	16.55	1	4	6/56
1972/3	Rhodesia Invitation XI	11	20	2	870	131	48.33	2	4	21	1049	60	17.48	2	4	9/71
1973	G.L.	18	29	5	1475	152	61.45	6	4	17	684	32	21.37	–	1	6/41
1973/4	Rhodesia Invitation XI	12	22	1	686	110	32.66	1	5	10	1117	47	23.76	–	–	4/42
1974	G.L.	19	33	3	1033	157	34.43	2	6	10	776	47	16.51	–	1	5/29
1974/5	Rhodesia	2	4	0	161	68	40.25	–	2	2	54	4	13.50	–	–	2/21
1975	G.L.	4	8	0	220	64	27.50	–	3	10	257	7	36.71	–	–	4/29
1975/6	Rhodesia	8	14	1	468	121*	36.00	1	2	3	373	10	37.30	–	–	4/109
1976	G.L.	21	38	3	1209	131	34.54	1	8	14	1908	68	28.05	2	3	7/82
1976/7	Natal	8	12	1	261	59	23.72	–	3	7	936	59	15.86	2	7	7/77
1977	G.L.	21	33	2	857	115	27.64	2	3	17	1967	109	18.04	1	9	7/35
1977/8	Natal	1	2	0	44	31	22.00	–	–	–	53	4	13.25	–	–	4/53
1978	G.L.	21	36	3	1655	203	50.15	3	7	11	1649	69	23.89	1	2	7/45
1978/9	Natal	2	4	1	86	55*	28.66	–	1	1	211	18	14.72	1	2	6/25
1979	G.L.	21	36	4	1241	122	38.78	3	7	11	1532	81	18.91	1	7	8/30
1979/80	Natal	8	14	0	420	110	30.00	1	1	5	870	45	19.33	1	2	7/29
1980	G.L.	19	33	2	1081	134*	34.87	1	7	17	931	51	18.25	1	3	7/16
1980/81	Natal	8	11	1	257	61	25.70	–	2	6	462	24	19.25	–	–	4/43
Total		374	626	55	21082	254	36.92	47	105	306	25164	1357	19.07	14	67	9/71

Best performances in Rest of World vs England 1970 series

Batsmen	'T'	R	Ave	Bowlers	'T'	W	Ave
Garry Sobers	5	588	73.50	Eddie Barlow	5	20	19.80
Ray Illingworth	5	476	52.89	Mike Procter	5	15	23.93
Mike Procter	5	292	48.66	Garry Sobers	5	21	21.52
Geoff Boycott	2	260	65.00	Tony Greig	5	11	26.18

WSC World XI batting averages

Player	M	I	NO	Runs	HS	Ave	100	50	0s
Barry Richards	2	3	1	166	101*	83.00	1	0	0
Zaheer Abbas	3	5	0	204	91	40.80	0	1	0
Mike Procter	3	5	0	171	66	34.20	0	2	0
Majid Khan	2	3	0	101	77	33.66	0	1	0
Clive Rice	3	5	0	151	83	32.20	0	1	0
Imran Khan	3	5	2	90	24	30.00	0	0	0
Javed Miandad	2	3	0	89	59	29.66	0	1	0
Asif Iqbal	3	5	0	142	107	28.40	1	0	0
Derek Underwood	3	4	1	42	32	14.00	0	0	0
Garth le Roux	3	4	1	34	33*	11.33	0	0	2
Alan Knott	3	4	1	33	11	11.00	0	0	0
Dennis Amiss	1	2	0	6	6	3.00	0	0	1
Tony Greig	1	1	0	0	0	0.00	0	0	1
Eddie Barlow	1	2	0	0	0	0.00	0	0	2

WSC World XI bowling averages

Player	M	I	O	M	R	W	BBI	BBM	Ave	Econ	SR	5	10	Ct
Garth le Roux	3	6	108.00	22	270	17	5/39	9/101	15.88	2.50	38.1	2	0	1
Mike Procter	3	6	57.1	12	167	9	3/33	4/78	18.55	2.92	38.1	0	0	2
Imran Khan	3	6	87.2	23	227	12	4/30	6/67	18.91	2.59	43.6	0	0	2
Derek Underwood	3	6	125.0	50	231	11	4/59	6/95	21.00	1.84	68.1	0	0	1

At the end of the World Cricket Series, several writers convened to pick their best XI from the series. The teams make for interesting reading.

Critics combined team:
Barry Richards (SA/World), Gordon Greenidge (West Indies), Viv Richards (West Indies), Greg Chappell (Australia), Lawrence Rowe (West Indies), Mike Procter (SA/World), Alan Knott (Eng/World, wicketkeeper), Andy Roberts (West Indies), Dennis Lillee (Australia), Joel Garner (West Indies), Derek Underwood (Eng/World)

Critics Australian XI
Bruce Laird, Kepler Wessels, Ian Chappell (capt), Greg Chappell, Martin Kent, David Hookes, Rod Marsh (wicketkeeper), Ray Bright, Max Walker, Dennis Lillee, Len Pascoe, Jeff Thomson (12th man)

Critics West Indies XI:
Gordon Greenidge, Roy Fredericks, Viv Richards, Lawrence Rowe, Clive Lloyd (capt), Collis King, Deryck Murray (wicketkeeper), Andy Roberts, Michael Holding, Joel Garner, Colin Croft, Albert Padmore (12th man)

Critics World XI:
Barry Richards (SA), Majid Khan (Pakistan), Zaheer Abbas (Pakistan), Asif Iqbal (Pakistan), Tony Greig (England-capt), Clive Rice (SA), Mike Procter (SA), Alan Knott (England-wicketkeeper), Imran Khan (Pakistan), Garth le Roux (SA), Derek Underwood (England), Dennis Amiss (England–12th man)

Finally, just a bit of devil's advocate. Combining my games of stature for the Rest of the World and the World Series, but putting aside my seven Tests, would also make for interesting reading. My bowling average doesn't change too much, but my batting average shoots up to 40!

Bowler	Official career			Adjusted for Packer, World XIs (1970 and 1972-73 and depleted teams)		
	T	W	Ave	'T'	W	Ave
Mike Procter	7	41	15.02	16	70	17.14
Joel Garner	58	259	20.93	63	281	21.69
Imran Khan	88	362	22.81	93	387	22.68
Michael Holding	60	249	23.69	69	284	23.58
Dennis Lillee	70	355	23.92	88	446	24.16
Colin Croft	27	125	23.30	32	146	24.76
Bob Willis	90	325	25.20	84	305	25.34
Wayne Daniel	10	36	25.28	17	50	25.34

Player	M	Runs	Ave	Ct	M	Runs	Ave	Ct
Desmond Haynes	116	7,487	42.29	18	118	7,375	40.75	18
Keith Stackpole	43	2,807	37.42	7	48	3,297	39.25	9
Gundappa Viswanath	91	6,080	41.93	14	74	4,592	37.64	10
Tony Greig	58	3,599	40.43	8	70	3,946	37.23	8
Imran Khan	88	3,807	37.69	6	93	3,934	36.77	6
David Hookes	23	1,306	34.36	1	35	2,076	35.79	3
Ian Botham	102	5,200	33.54	14	96	4,909	33.86	14
Mike Procter	7	226	25.11	0	16	700	33.33	0
Kapil Dev	131	5,248	31.05	8	119	4,707	29.79	7
Chetan Chauhan	40	2,084	31.57	0	24	1,144	26.60	0
Ray Illingworth	61	1,836	23.24	0	66	2,244	25.50	0

Bibliography

Border, Allan. *Cricket As I See It*, published November 2014, Allen and Unwin Publishers

Ponting, Ricky. *At the Close of Play*, published June 2014, Harpersport Publishers

Online sources:

http://www.espncricinfo.com/ci/content/image/index.html?object=46793

http://www.cricketcountry.com/articles/what-if-packer-supertests-and-world-xi-matches-of-the-1970s-had-been-official-tests-194978

Index